Windows 11 for Seniors

The Most Exhaustive Step-by-Step Guide to Learn how to use Windows Effortlessly with Illustrated Instructions and Simple Explanations.

Lukas Worley

WINDOWS 11 FOR SENIOR

TABLE OF CONTENTS

TABLE OF CONTENTS

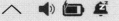

PREFACE

DEAR READER

Before we dive into the wonderful world of Windows 11, I would like to thank you for your purchase. There are so many books on this subject, and your preference fills me with pride and satisfaction. I hope that I can repay your trust by conveying to you, with this book, all the passion I have for Windows and help you learn the necessary notions that will immediately allow you to use it effortlessly.

Through years of using Windows, I've noticed that there are limited resources available written by individuals who use Windows 11 on a daily basis, providing comprehensive guidance on optimizing its usage. Furthermore, Windows 11 offers numerous opportunities and employment prospects, making it the most widely utilized operating system by individuals.

This is one of the reasons that prompted me to write this book and create an active community that helps each other. My dream and mission is to create a series of books on all the major IT solutions used in large companies, so that you already know what awaits you out there if you decide to make this passion your job. To quote Confucius, "Do the work you love, and you will not work a day in your life." Believe me, that's exactly right.

Scan this QR code to get a free bonus and access my Facebook community, where users from different parts of the world ask questions and get answers to all doubts and problems about the IT world, such as Windows, Linux, Office 365, Teams, Excel, Word, and more.

I'm waiting for you inside, where you'll find many interesting insights.

This book is written for those who want to approach this world out of simple curiosity or to increase their cultural background. It's designed and written for users at any starting level of knowledge, from beginners to more advanced users. While some concepts might seem trivial or superfluous to those with a minimum mastery of the subject, going over some notions might still be a good exercise. Also, I would like to ask for your help in augmenting and improving my work. It will be quick and easy for you, but it's essential for me. If you could leave an objective review of a few lines on Amazon (or the portal where you bought the book), it would be crucial for me. Thank you very much indeed!

 WINDOWS 11 FOR SENIOR

WHO I AM

Let's start with introductions. My name is Lukas Worley, and I was born on November 23, 1985, in Philadelphia. I was lucky enough to have a father who was a systems administrator at a small family-run company, where he was in charge of the IT department. Since he often worked after hours, I grew up with a computer at home and heard terms that were very cutting-edge for the time, such as network interconnections, routers, switches, etc.

My destiny was already sealed, and this world increasingly fascinated me. I pursued technical studies, culminating in a computer engineering degree and a network and telecommunications specialization.

After graduation, I devoted myself to the cybersecurity world, which has exploded in recent years. Every new technology fascinates me, and thanks to my work as an IT consultant, I also have the opportunity to travel extensively. I lived in Italy for a semester to participate in a master's program in data cybersecurity at the Polytechnic University of Turin (where I also learned Italian) and three months in Bristol for a specialization course on network perimeter security (Palo Alto and Checkpoint firewalls).

For several years, I worked as a systems administrator for prestigious companies (especially in the automotive field), then as the IT manager for the EMEA region of a major internet service provider. Now, as a freelance consultant with more time to devote to my passions, I have decided to share my technical knowledge and expertise through a series of books on technology. Perhaps one of my biggest regrets was not pursuing an academic career to become a university lecturer because I believe that teaching is something truly extraordinary—the bond that is created with students and the satisfaction of seeing those people succeed. This is one of the reasons why you are reading this book because years later, I want to try to realize this small dream of mine in an alternative way.

I hope that the journey of this and the other books I will write is fascinating

 WINDOWS 11 FOR SENIOR

and can provide you with the answers you are seeking. Let's begin our journey immediately, welcome aboard.

 WINDOWS 11 FOR SENIOR

INTRODUCTION

Welcome, and thank you for choosing this book!

If you're here, it's because you've decided to learn more about this fantastic operating system.

Since the dawn of the first electronic computers, Windows has always played a leading role in the development of operating systems. An operating system is the software that manages a computer's resources and provides an interface between the user and the system's hardware. It controls access to resources, such as memory, processors, and input/output devices, and also manages background processes such as file and network management.

The history of Windows is full of incredible features and innovations, but it has also had its share of flops (Windows ME, for example).

The next major version of Microsoft Windows will be called Windows 11, and it will be the version that comes after Windows 10. On October 5, 2021, Microsoft launched Windows 11 as a free update that could be installed on compatible laptops, desktop computers, and bigger tablets.

However, Windows 11 has stricter hardware compatibility than Windows 10, which means that certain older devices won't be supported or able to upgrade to Windows 11. Windows 11 has an updated and streamlined user interface designed to be more user-friendly and aesthetically beautiful. Microsoft hopes that this will encourage more productivity and creativity among its users.

Let's take a look together at the evolution of this software over time, enjoy your reading, and happy studying.

 WINDOWS 11 FOR SENIOR

The Evolution of Windows

The operating system plays a crucial mediator between the user and the computer. The software creates a setting where the user may carry out his tasks without being aware of or concerned with the underlying computer hardware mechanics. As a result, we may say that the operating system is the software responsible for controlling the computer's hardware.

Microsoft is a key player in the market for operating systems, which some vendors now populate. In 1985, Microsoft released the Windows operating system for IBM PCs and compatibles. The installation process for Windows begins with this step. Microsoft chose to call its OS Windows because of its focus on creating intuitive, graphical user interfaces. According to recent estimates, 8 out of 10 computers use Microsoft Windows as their operating system, while Linux and Mac share the remaining portion of the market. The father of this operating system, as you are well aware, is Bill Gates. He came from a wealthy family and was fortunate enough to attend one of the best schools and have a computer at his disposal. It may seem like a no-brainer to you, but at that time, a computer was the size of an entire room and was not exactly affordable. Because of this opportunity, Mr. Gates had the chance to fall in love with this world. When he was only 15 years old, he won a scholarship for designing software to manage class schedules. The scholarship was for about $500, which was an absurd amount of money at the time. Gates was a visionary, and even at such a young age, he began to plan the creation of his own company that would develop software.

The turning point came when Gates' mother set him up with an important executive at IBM, which was already a solid and important company. Bill was able to get a meeting and even a contract with IBM. In fact, his newly created company, Microsoft, was to create the software for all IBM employees' computers. It's worth noting that Gates did not have such advanced and complex software available, so he ordered it and had it developed by another programmer, keeping him in the dark about his true intentions. When the software was ready, it was branded as MS-DOS and sold to IBM.

 WINDOWS 11 FOR SENIOR

However, here's where Gates' real insight and entrepreneurial prowess came into play. He proposed to have $3 for every installation of the software, forever. IBM thought it was making a good deal, but within only 4 months of the launch of the personal computer, 60,000 units were sold.

Windows 1
Launching on November 20, 1985, Windows 1 was developed and released by Microsoft. It was a lightweight 16-bit OS that required less than 1 MB of storage. For the first time, an operating system was created with a graphical user interface. This OS was developed for IBM-compatible hardware. This operating system is optimized for mouse-based actions, including clicking, dragging, dropping, and moving.

Windows 2
A new version of Windows, Windows 2, was released on December 9, 1987. This OS is also a 16-bit operating system. The speed and visual quality of the OS were two of its primary focuses in this update. Additionally, this OS supported keyboard shortcuts. New features included 16-color VGA graphics, expanding and shrinking windows, and overlay applications. Windows 2.0 also supported Microsoft's initial versions of Word and Excel for Windows.

Windows 3
On May 22, 1990, Windows 3 was released. This new edition of Windows brought significant improvements. One of the many improvements was the introduction of improved icons. With the capability of displaying 256 colors, the user interface became brighter and more visually appealing. Additionally, this release allowed MS-DOS programs to be launched inside Windows. To assist users with various tasks, Windows introduced several managers such as the Program Manager, Downloader, Panel, and Print Manager. A significant upgrade to Windows 3 was also released, often referred to as Windows 3.1. This update's primary selling point was its native networking functionality, which aided in the development of intranet by linking several computers. True Type fonts were also added in this release, along with the ability to utilize Windows as a publishing platform.
The first CD-ROM release of Windows was version 3.1.

 WINDOWS 11 FOR SENIOR

Windows 95

Codenamed "Chicago," Microsoft's next major OS was under development after Windows 3.1. On August 24, 1995, the public was presented with this operating system for the first time. The first Start button, Start menu, and taskbar debuted in Windows 95. It was also the first to provide built-in support for dial-up Internet access and the revolutionary notion of plug-and-play. A 32-bit OS, Windows 95 improved multimedia capabilities. However, it could also be used in 16-bit and 32-bit modes. This release required both 4 MB of RAM and 55 MB of hard drive space. Additionally, it included the pioneering Internet Explorer browser.

Windows 98

The project's debut occurred on June 25, 1998. This release included DVD and USB disk reading functionality. Memphis was chosen as the codename for this particular release. You could choose between 32-bit and 16-bit versions of this release.

 WINDOWS 11 FOR SENIOR

Microsoft developed new capabilities, including Disk Cleanup, Windows Update, support for multiple monitors, internet sharing, etc., and included them in this release. For this release, you needed between 16 and 24 MB of RAM and between 140 and 355 MB of hard drive space. It was also compatible with CD and DVD ROM drives. This version was the first to include Microsoft's new fast-launch functionality.

Windows 2000

Due to its focus on the needs of businesses, the Windows 2000 Professional edition was created to replace older versions of Windows on all office computers. This revision became available in February of 2000. The set included four Windows editions: Business, Server, Expert Server, and Advanced Server.

The encrypting NTFS 3.0 file system was also introduced in this release. Plug-and-play functionality, including complete ACPI and Windows Driver Model compatibility, was a major focus for this release. This development also introduced layered windows with the capacity for transparency. This release requires a server space of 5 GB and 256 MB of RAM.

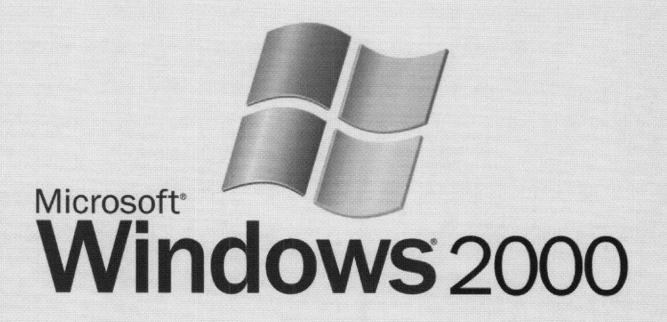

Windows XP

Released on October 25, 2001, this version of Windows has been around for over two decades and is one of Microsoft's best-selling products. It was developed using the Windows NT Kernel with the general public in mind and was the first version of Windows that wasn't built on MS-DOS. Windows XP was available in two primary editions, Professional and Home, and had both 32-bit and 64-bit versions.

Microsoft also included a CD-burning utility with the program. Windows XP had a fresh new look with increased usage of alpha blending effects, dropped shadows, and various visual styles. It introduced a new two-column Start menu design with shortcuts to commonly used programs, recently accessed files, and the classic drop-down "All Programs" section. A single application's windows could now be collapsed into a single button on the taskbar, with a popup menu showing each window's location.

In addition to adding a firewall to protect internet connections, Windows XP had other new networking capabilities. Microsoft released three service packs for Windows XP, called Windows XP Updates: Workability 1, Service Pack 2, and Service Pack 3. Microsoft's support for Windows XP continued until April of 2014, making it its longest-lived OS.

Windows Vista

It was released on January 30, 2007. Windows Vista introduced a new aesthetic that emphasized transparency, search, and security. The codename for this release was Microsoft's Longhorn. The applications and permissions under user account management were also upgraded to provide maximum security in this release. To function properly, this version required 1 GB of RAM, 40 GB of HDD capacity, and a CPU speed of 1 GHz. Microsoft also included some user-friendly enhancements in Windows Vista, such as the Windows Shell, Windows searches, and the Windows Operating system. Additionally, Microsoft included DirectX 10 with Vista to improve the gaming experience on PCs.

 WINDOWS 11 FOR SENIOR

Windows 7

Microsoft officially unveiled Windows 7 on October 22, 2009. Blackcomb is Microsoft's official name for this update. In addition, it was an incremental improvement to Windows XP and was designed primarily for wireless devices like laptops, which had begun to displace desktops. Windows 7 was available in a total of six different flavors, including "home basic," "home premium," "professional," and "ultimate." Users flocked to this OS after discovering its innovative new capabilities. Due to its superior performance, reliability, and user-friendliness, Windows 7 quickly surpassed Windows Vista as the preferred update for both home and commercial customers. A 32-bit and 64-bit release were also available. It required 20 GB of hard drive space in addition to 2 GB of RAM for the 64-bit version and 1 GB of RAM for the 32-bit version.

 WINDOWS 11 FOR SENIOR

Windows 8

The digital world is shifting more and more to mobile, and Windows is trying to introduce a new operating system that can adapt well to new devices such as tablets and smartphones. However, expectations for this new OS that was supposed to be revolutionary have not been met. The new user interface (called METRO, based on a "tile" interface) caused a lot of confusion for users accustomed to the classic Windows interface, but the biggest issue was the lack of compatibility with different applications, as well as software and drivers.

Windows 8 was released on October 26, 2012. With its tile-based start menu and absence of the traditional "Start" button, this OS fundamentally altered the operating system architecture and user experience. It works well on mobile devices with touch screens like tablets, Windows phones, and laptops. Windows apps can now be downloaded via Microsoft's Windows Store. Users can choose between a 64-bit version and a 32-bit version based on the capabilities of their computers. Microsoft also included new features in this release, such as product testing, a status bar, remote desktop, and more. Microsoft also included UEFI support and the new "Hybrid Boot" option, both of which speed up the boot process. Windows 8 requires a minimum of 4 GB of RAM and 20 GB of available disk space.

 WINDOWS 11 FOR SENIOR

Windows 8.1

Only a year after the disappointing release of Windows 8, an update was released: Windows 8.1. Microsoft attempted to learn from their mistakes and gathered user feedback to improve the previous operating system. The "Start" button, which had been eliminated in Windows 8's METRO interface, was reinserted. Overall, Windows 8.1 was seen as a step forward from Windows 8, introducing important new features in terms of customization and making significant efforts to make the operating system more accessible and user-friendly. However, some users experienced compatibility problems and needed to purchase the Pro version to take advantage of some features.

Window 10

Microsoft Windows 10 is the most recent version of the Windows operating system. Last updated on July 29th, 2015. Many new features were introduced with Windows 10, including support for universal applications, an extension of Metro-style programs, the ability to choose between a mouse- and touch-based interface, and the retention of the classic start button. Windows 10 needs a minimum of 4 GB of RAM and 32 GB of available hard drive space. As a bonus, Microsoft made it work with touch- and mouse-based devices. The newest version of DirectX, 12, is compatible with Windows 10. Windows Defender Antivirus and Microsoft's new Multi-Factor Authentication system are two examples of how Microsoft has bolstered Windows' security. Microsoft Edge, the new web browser in Windows 10, is far quicker than Internet Explorer, Microsoft's previous browser. Microsoft is continuing to work on Windows 10.

What Is Windows 11

Windows 11 is the latest version of the Microsoft Windows operating system, which was officially released on the night of October 4-5, 2021. The official unveiling took place on June 24, 2021, via Microsoft's official YouTube channel. Windows 11 is the natural evolution of Windows 10, and if you are already using it, you will have no problem transitioning to this great new operating system.
I have to be honest, I am excited about Windows 11. Before writing this book, I wanted to test it thoroughly, and I must say that it is one of the best operating systems Microsoft has ever created. I really like the graphics, which are eye-catching and reminiscent of (in a good way) Macs, with the central taskbar featuring very large icons.

Windows 11 was created with the promise of making the operating system much easier to use for end-users, as it is more oriented towards the mobile world. It also includes the ability to run Android applications in emulation mode.
Windows 11, typically the home version, will be preinstalled on new personal computers, laptops, and tablets using the PC operating system. You are eligible for this offer if you bought an older system in 2017 or later. There is a possibility that you may update to Windows 11. It seems doubtful that older PCs will be capable of supporting Windows 11, especially if they are running Windows 10. Depending on their needs, customers may choose between the Home and Pro versions of Windows 11.

The Home Version of Windows 11
It is compatible with desktop computers, laptops, and even tablets. This version is geared toward the typical person who uses a computer at home. It is the version you most likely have if you purchased your laptop or tablet device from a retailer specializing in computers. A list of the features included in this version can be seen below.

 WINDOWS 11 FOR SENIOR

Windows 11 Pro

It is the same as the home version, except it has some extra features tailored to corporate settings and advanced users. In the right-hand column of this list, you will get a rundown of the features exclusive to Windows 11 Professional.

What's New in Windows 11

Windows 11 features a completely redesigned user interface with transparent windows, updated icons, and fonts, and rounded edges throughout the operating system. The most visible change is that the start menu and taskbar have been moved to the center of the screen. However, for die-hard Windows users, the option to position the taskbar to the left is still available. It is worth noting that the centered method is simpler, as the start button and applications are positioned to be more readily accessible when using a mouse.

Windows 11 also reintroduces widgets, allowing users to install widgets for various topics such as weather, photos, news, stocks, and more. A new notification center combines a calendar with it. There are several new capabilities for multiple or virtual desktops, including the ability to switch between desktops by clicking a button on the taskbar. You can also have different backgrounds for each desktop and give each desktop a name and arrange their order on the desktop bar at the bottom of the screen.

Windows Search has been condensed into an icon resembling a magnifying glass, allowing users to search for applications, files, and settings. Brand new snap layouts make it easier to multitask, allowing you to easily rearrange windows on your screen using various preset layouts. The user interface of File Explorer has also been updated to give it a more contemporary look, with a simplified ribbon along the top containing several frequently used tools. Additionally, you will see several new icons for devices, files, and folders.

Features of Windows 11

Among many, some of the features of Windows 11 are:

Settings App
The Windows 11 Settings App is a built-in application within the Windows 11 operating system that allows users to personalize and configure various system settings. It is an enhanced version of the Settings app found in Windows 10, featuring a redesigned user interface to align with the new Windows 11 design.

With the Settings App, users can manage network settings, including Wi-Fi and Bluetooth connections, customize audio preferences, adjust screen brightness, personalize system appearance and themes, modify privacy options, manage user accounts and passwords, update the operating system, install new applications, handle device and connected peripherals, and much more.

The Windows 11 Settings App aims to provide a more intuitive and user-friendly experience compared to previous Windows versions, offering improved consistency in design and organization of settings. The app features a tabbed interface that categorizes different settings, making it simpler to locate and access the desired options.

Microsoft Store
The Microsoft Store is a digital distribution platform for apps, games, movies, music, books, and other content designed for devices running the Windows operating system. It serves as Microsoft's official store for Windows users, similar to app stores available on other operating systems like iOS and Android.

Through the Microsoft Store, users can browse, discover, and download a wide range of applications and content to enhance their Windows experience. The store offers a diverse selection of apps developed by Microsoft, independent developers, and third-party companies, ensuring a variety of choices and opportunities for personalizing Windows devices.

 WINDOWS 11 FOR SENIOR

The Microsoft Store also prioritizes security by providing a secure environment for developers to publish their applications. Each app undergoes verification processes to ensure compliance with Microsoft's rigorous security and quality standards. This ensures that users can confidently download and install apps without the risk of encountering malware or malicious software.

Furthermore, the Microsoft Store offers convenient features such as automatic app updates, seamless account and license management, and support for various Windows platforms, including PCs, tablets, mobile devices, and Xbox game consoles. This allows users to easily keep their apps up to date and enjoy a consistent experience across their Windows devices.

Android Integration

Windows 11 has introduced a new feature called "Windows Integration with Android," which enables greater synergy between the Windows operating system and Android devices.

Through Windows Integration with Android, users can connect their Android device to their Windows computer and take advantage of some interconnected features. For example, Android phone notifications can be accessed directly on the Windows desktop, allowing users to view and respond to messages, incoming calls, and other notifications without having to pick up the phone. Windows integration with Android also supports file and photo sharing between the computer and the Android device, making it easy to transfer data and access desired content.

Widgets

Windows 11 widgets are small, interactive, and informative elements that can be placed on the desktop or the main screen of the operating system. Widgets offer a convenient way to display useful information at a glance, such as news updates, weather forecasts, calendar events, task reminders, currently playing music, and more.

What Are the Main Components of a PC?

Keeping your PC running smoothly and for as long as possible requires regular maintenance and updates. Like any electrical device, computer hardware ultimately fails after extensive usage. There are several potential causes for a computer to slow down, and the vast majority of them can be addressed without risking damage to the machine's internals. However, in more severe cases, upgrading is usually the best option. The five most important parts of a computer are as follows:

Motherboard

The motherboard, the central circuit board that connects and supports all the other parts, is always first on any comprehensive computer parts list. From desktop computers to portable laptops, it can be found everywhere. A powerful motherboard will have several expansion slots to add more parts to your computer (e.g., RAM, graphics card, etc.). Motherboards come in various form factors (generic features, including circuitry layout, overall size, number of ports, etc.), and only certain motherboard types can fit into certain computer cases/chassis, particularly for modifiable desktops. Instead, laptops employ specialized motherboards with pre-soldered hardware components permanently attached to their circuit boards. Due to their portable nature and lightweight construction, only certain components, such as memory and storage, can be changed in a laptop. When a computer's motherboard is damaged, the whole machine stops working. Due to the intricate nature of the motherboard's circuitry and wiring, a failing component there can immediately render your computer inoperable and even cause damage to other components. While desktop motherboards can be swapped out, laptops cannot, so if yours goes bad, you'll need to purchase a new computer.

Central Processing Unit (CPU)

A computer's "brain" is its central processing unit (CPU), the processor. The central processing unit (CPU) executes your computer's complex algorithms and programs. Nowadays, it's rare to find a computer without several central processing units (CPUs), which exponentially increase processing speed and

guarantee instantaneous responses from your program and the web. Multi-core processors are specialized CPUs with more than one central processing unit (CPU).

For instance, the high-end Intel® CoreTM i7-12850HX CPU has 16 separate cores collaborating to perform computational tasks, letting you run many programs simultaneously without overwhelming your machine. By overclocking, you may receive marginal gains in performance from your processors. However, remember that doing so has hazards that might permanently harm your CPU. Remember that a faulty CPU may cripple an otherwise fully functional PC.

Graphics Processing Unit (GPU)

The graphics processing unit (GPU) is the computer's component for graphical processing and high-resolution visuals. Virtually all modern media relies heavily on graphical representations and effects, which need the use of a graphics processing unit (GPU) to be read and reproduced by your computer. Certain high-end CPUs, often high-end laptops with an emphasis on lightweight portability and usage, may also have rudimentary GPUs incorporated in them. The best GPUs, however, are often reserved for video games because of their ability to process massive amounts of 3D graphics data without slowing down or causing any latency. CPU and GPU are complementary while playing games. The graphics processing unit (GPU) handles the visuals and quality of the game, while the central processing unit (CPU) handles the data and statistics generated by the game itself. Any issues, including the dreaded "black screen of death," might be caused by a malfunctioning GPU. A GPU being lost is a nightmare due to GPU chip shortages.

Random Access Memory (RAM)

Random Access Memory (RAM) is the most well-known type of computer memory used for storing information and data. A RAM device stores frequently accessed data and codes in a buffer, making them immediately available when the relevant application or app is launched. All information saved in RAM is cleared when the computer is turned off since it is a volatile memory. Because of this, the next time you use the device, it will be ready to start loading data much more rapidly because it already has everything it needs to get started.

Almost any common computer, including small laptops, can have extra RAM installed by purchasing a newer RAM device with increased data storage capacity, often referred to as a RAM stick. However, depending on your computer activities, you may not utilize all RAM, so you should know how much RAM suits your PC based on its primary usage (work, gaming, etc.). A broken RAM stick may or may not immediately render your computer inoperable, but it will eventually cause issues such as software crashes, abnormal reduction in RAM, and a failure to load.

Repository

A storage device is a piece of hardware with memory that may be used to store data, such as programs and files. In contrast to RAM, data stored on a storage device is stored in non-volatile memory, meaning it will remain intact even if the computer is powered off (unless manually deleted or uninstalled).

Two main forms of internal storage used in personal computers are hard disk drives (HDDs) and solid-state drives (SSDs). While solid-state drives (SSDs) are better than HDDs in almost every way, they are also more costly. SATA connections connect these devices to your PC, but larger servers and workstations should use SAS cables instead. USB flash drives and portable hard disk drives are only two examples of additional storage options. However, these add-ons are not built into PCs. Instead, they use a different connection method, such as a USB cable or an external hard drive, to link to the computer. Storage devices don't affect your computer's startup time, but applications like Chrome and Word are loaded from the hard drive or solid-state drive immediately after booting. File corruption might occur if the operation is interrupted by a damaged storage device. It's inconvenient to reinstall Windows or reformat your computer and a new hard drive if that happens.

Windows 11 System Requirements

At the unveiling of Windows 11 and upon the release of its first beta version, one of the biggest concerns among users was the announcement from Windows that the new operating system would only be compatible with machines that met certain minimum requirements:

- **Processor** - 1 gigahertz (GHz) or faster with 2 or more cores on a compatible 64-bit processor or System on a Chip (SoC).
- **RAM** - 4 gigabyte (GB).
- **Storage** - 64 GB or larger storage device
- **System firmware** - UEFI, Secure Boot capable.
- **TPM** - Trusted Platform Module (TPM) version 2.0
- **Graphics card** - Compatible with DirectX 12 or later with WDDM 2.0 driver.
- **Display** – A greater than 9" diagonally, 8 bits per color channel.
- **Internet connection and Microsoft account** - For all Windows 11 editions, internet access is required to perform updates and to download and take advantage of some features. A Microsoft account is required for some features.
- **CPU** – Only some CPUs are compatible with Windows 11.

Find the full list here

These stringent requirements inevitably triggered much puzzlement and criticism, as most of the computers available to users would be incompatible. The biggest question raised was this: If Windows 11 is going to be more powerful than Windows 10 with the same amount of resources, why can't I install it on my PC where Windows 10 runs just fine? It's a fair question. I tried to provide my personal answer, which is that Microsoft made this choice to increase the security level of the new operating system. A new computer will undoubtedly enhance performance and not have inherent security flaws in the hardware/software that an attacker can exploit. This may not necessarily be the real motivation, but it is the only one that makes sense to me.

However, Microsoft being a company that is very attentive to user criticism, and mainly because it perceived the possibility of cutting off 70% of potential customers (which would have been a resounding flop), Microsoft itself backtracked and published a tutorial (in fact, there are several ways) on how to install Windows 11 on PCs that do not meet the minimum system requirements.

 WINDOWS 11 FOR SENIOR

Do you want to know how to install Windows without the minimum requirements?

Here it is, scan this QR Code-->

If you have trouble installing Windows, don't worry. You can contact me via email, and I will try to help you (or someone from my team). You can find my email here, where you can also download a free eBook with many tips on how to keep your Windows (whether 11 or 10) always running fast and performing well.

 WINDOWS 11 FOR SENIOR

QUIZ
INTRODUCTION

1 - Which version was the first to include Microsoft's new fast-launch functionality?

A)   Window XP
B)   Window 98
C)   Window 12

2 - What is METRO?

A)   Primary storage options
B)   A new user interface introduced in Windows 8
C)   A new application of Windows 11

3 - All information saved in ..... is cleared when the computer is turned off:

A)   RAM
B)   ROM
C)   Hard disk

4 - Which Window needs a minimum of 4 GB of RAM and 32 GB of available hard drive space?

A)   Window 10
B)   Window 11
C)   Window XP

 WINDOWS 11 FOR SENIOR

5 - What kind of firmware must my pc have to support Windows 11?
A) Legacy
B) UEFI

6 - In which version of Windows was CORTANA introduced?
A) Windows 98
B) Windows 10
C) Windows 11
D) Windows 8.1

7 - Both 32-bit and 64-bit editions are available of:
A)   Window 1
B)   Window 3
C)   Window XP

Answers

1.   B
2.   B
3.   A
4.   A
5.   B
6.   C
7.   C

CHAPTER 1
WAYS TO INSTALL (OR UPGRADE TO) WINDOWS 11

After having walked through the evolution of the Microsoft Windows operating system together and analyzed the main innovations and changes introduced, let's see how to install Windows 11 on our devices. There are different methods to do this, and below we will go step-by-step through the most popular ones, namely installation via Windows Update or installation on a new PC. As is always the case, especially in the second scenario, something may not go smoothly, but in this case, all you have to do is contact me and a specialist from my team will be happy to help you. The idea of this book and future ones is to create a great community of people helping each other.

Suppose you are running a fully licensed version of Windows 10 on your computer, and your computer is compatible with Windows 11. In that case, you will automatically get the Windows 11 upgrade at no additional cost. If you plan an upgrade, check that your computer satisfies the requirements below.
Two things that should be kept in mind. You will want a device equipped with a trusted platform module version 2.0. (TPM 2.0). A trusted platform module (TPM) is a chip often attached to the motherboard. It is used to verify a personal computer (PC) or laptop by storing passwords, digital certificates, or encryption keys in a safe place where malware cannot access or tamper with them. If you bought your computer after 2017, there is a good chance that this functionality will already be installed.

You should be able to check this out in the device manager.

 WINDOWS 11 FOR SENIOR

Device manager may be accessed by right-clicking the start button and choosing that option from the context menu.

1.1 Installing from Windows Update

If Windows 10 is currently your operating system, upgrading to Windows 11 will be very easy. All you need to do is upgrade via Windows Update, as we discussed in the previous chapter. One of the improvements made in Windows 11 is the simplicity of the first installation and configuration process.

First, ensure that you're connected to the internet (either via cable or Wi-Fi) and that your battery is charged. This may seem like a trivial tip, but even the most experienced people have occasionally started updates with a dead battery, and it's not advisable. Also, remember that to install Windows 11, you'll need a Microsoft account, so have your login credentials ready.

Next, click on the start icon and then on "**Settings**". This will take you to the Windows settings menu. From there, navigate to "**Update & Security**".

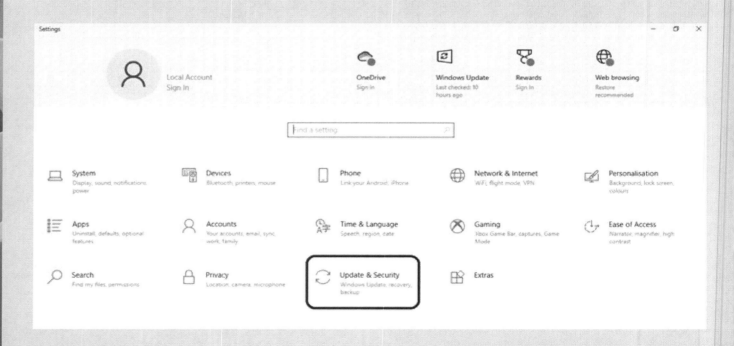

Click on Check for updates, and if our system requirements meet the minimum requirements for installing Windows 11 we will see the button to download and install Windows 11.

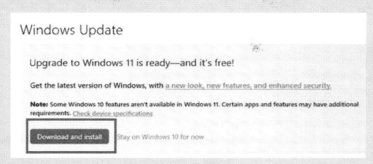

CAUTION. Before proceeding make a backup of all our files, better not to risk it!

When the download is complete, the system will ask you to make changes to your computer. Click "Accept" and wait until the installation is complete. During the download and installation phases, you will be asked to accept Microsoft's terms and conditions. Once everything is completed, you can click on the "Finish" button to finish the update process, which usually takes 30 to 60 minutes. After the installation, Windows will reboot itself and start with the new operating system. If this does not happen, restart the computer manually.

1.2 Perform a Clean Install

If you have a new PC and want to install Windows 11 or want to install it by formatting your current PC, you will first need to take some preliminary steps, which we can summarize as follows:

1. Check that your PC meets all the requirements to support Windows 11.
2. Download the ISO file.
3. Create a bootable flash drive with the new operating system.
4. Install the new operating system using this flash drive.

Let's take a closer look at each step described above:

Check that your PC meets all the requirements to support Windows 11.
To avoid any unpleasant surprises during installation, it is always a good idea to check that your PC meets the minimum requirements for installing the software. Microsoft provides us with a tool to perform this check, called the PC Health Check.

You can download it from this address, **just scan this QR code --->**

Once downloaded, install it by accepting the license terms, and when the installation is complete, start the tool by clicking end and leaving the check mark on Open PC Integrity check. Inside the tool you will have all the information about your PC and you only have to click on check now to get a report on all the specifications that windows 11 requires.

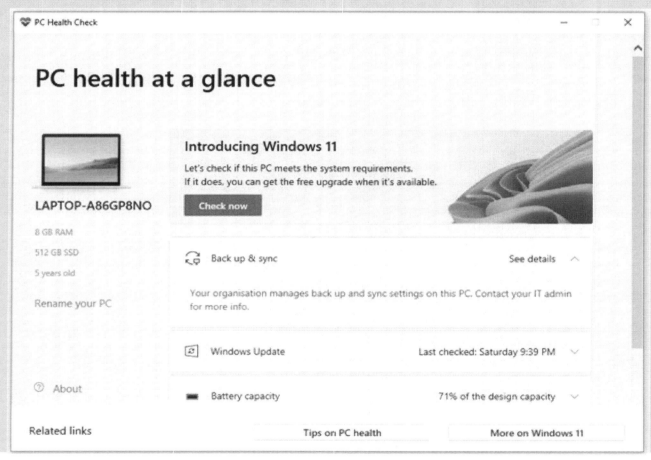

 WINDOWS 11 FOR SENIOR

You simply click on Check Now to verify the suitability of Windows 11 on your PC. Here, you have two options. Either the test was successful and your system is compatible with Windows 11, or your system does not meet the minimum requirements for Windows 11.

Scenario 1: Install Windows 11 on PCs that meet the minimum requirements

In this scenario, we have passed the check, so let's proceed with creating the bootable USB stick. I realize that for a novice person, this procedure might seem very complex.

That is why I will try to make the process as simple as possible.

✓	This PC supports Secure Boot.
✓	TPM 2.0 enabled on this PC. TPM: TPM 2.0
✓	There is at least 4 GB of system memory (RAM). System memory: 8 GB
✓	The system disk is 64 GB or larger. System storage: 512 GB

However, if you have any difficulties, feel free to contact me through Facebook (like my page) or email.

Download the ISO file and create a bootable Windows 11 flash drive.
We need to download two files: the ISO (available at this link) and the Rufus executable file, which in my opinion is the best program for creating a bootable USB stick.

- https://www.microsoft.com/software-download/windows11
- https://rufus.ie

To download the ISO, select the language you prefer and then click on "Download 64 bit" to download the ISO file (which will have the extension .ISO - we will explain later what a file extension means, for now just take note of this information). For Rufus, download the latest version and install it following the same steps used to install the integrity software.

 WINDOWS 11 FOR SENIOR

 Before you begin

Download Now

Create Windows 11 Installation Media

If you want to perform a reinstall or clean install of Windows 11 on a new or used PC, use this option to download the media creation tool to make a bootable USB or DVD.

 Before you begin

Download Now

Download Windows 11 Disk Image (ISO) for x64 devices

This option is for users that want to create a bootable installation media (USB flash drive, DVD) or create a virtual machine (.ISO file) to install Windows 11. This download is a multi-edition ISO which uses your product key to unlock the correct edition.

Windows 11 (multi-edition ISO for x64 devices) ⌄

Before you begin

Download

Start Rufus and insert the USB flash drive into the computer. Rufus will immediately recognize the USB stick, and all the parameters will be entered automatically by the software. The only thing you will have to do is click on the little icon with the disk (next to ISO Image) and select the .ISO file you had previously downloaded. After that, click on Start. You will be shown a warning informing you that all the data on the flash drive will be lost, so if you have files you need, **make a copy of them first.**

 WINDOWS 11 FOR SENIOR

At the end of the creation process, which takes an average of 7 to 10 minutes, you will have created your USB flash drive. It was simple, wasn't it?

Install the new operating system through this flash drive.
Now let's come to the more technical part where you may have a little more difficulty than in all the steps you have done so far. But you will see that together, we will be able to complete this procedure as well.

Restart your computer, and when it reboots, press the button to enter the BIOS, which is the first program you see when your PC reboots and before you see Windows (or your operating system in general) start up. But why do we need to enter the BIOS? Because by default, our PC boots using the software that is installed on our hard drive (which would be the previous version of Windows). We, on the other hand, want our PC to start from the bootable USB stick we created, so we have to tell the PC to change the boot order, putting not the hard drive but the USB stick on top.

To access the BIOS, there are several methods that depend on the type of computer you have. For example, to access the BIOS on my Fujitsu, I need to press the F2 key when I reboot. Other PCs, on the other hand, need the F8 key, while others need the CANC key.

When you are in the BIOS, look for the **BOOT** part and change the order by starting the PC from USB, then save and exit.

On exit, your PC will reboot and start the Windows 11 installation. Believe me, it is much easier than it sounds, and you are now ready to install Windows 11.

```
          Aptio Setup Utility - Copyright (C) 2012 American Megatrends, Inc.
   Main  Advanced  Server Mgmt  Boot  Security  Save & Exit  Power

  BIOS Information                                      This submenu provides details
  BIOS Vendor                     American Megatrends   on the system configuration
  Customized by                   Fujitsu
  Core Version                    4.6.5.6

▶ System Information

  System Language                 [English]

  System Date                     [Fri 01/02/2015]
  System Time                     [16:32:51]

  Access Level                    Administrator
                                                        ↔: Select Screen
                                                        ↑↓: Select Item
                                                        Enter: Select
                                                        +/-: Change Opt.
                                                        F1: General Help
                                                        F2: Previous Values
                                                        F3: Optimized Defaults
                                                        F4: Save & Exit
                                                        ESC: Exit
```

Scenario 2: Install Windows 11 on PCs that do not meet the minimum requirements

You bought your PC a few years ago and have never had any performance problems with Windows 10. You are fascinated by the possibility of upgrading to Windows 11, but when you try to upgrade, you unfortunately find that your computer does not meet the system requirements! Now what? Do you have to change your PC and spend a lot of money again?

NO! Don't worry. There are several ways to bypass this limitation and have Windows 11 running perfectly on your computer.

 WINDOWS 11 FOR SENIOR

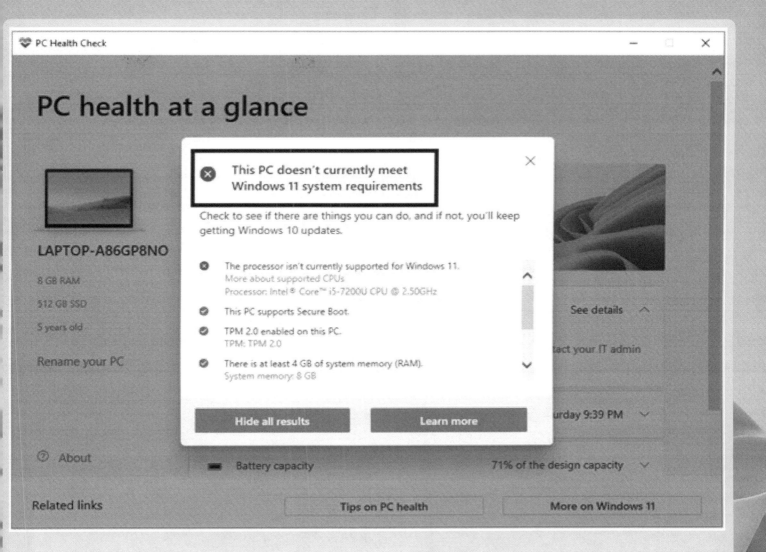

First, we need to figure out what is not compatible with the upgrade. Is TPM not enabled? Do you have an unsupported processor? Is Secure Boot not enabled? As you can see, the causes can be different, and each scenario has a different solution. To cover all the specific cases would really be too long, not least because some resolutions are within the reach of those with very advanced computer skills.

What I want you to understand in this subchapter is that even if your PC seems not to support Windows 11, there are ways to install it. In this case, on my old desktop PC, the processor is not supported. But to bypass this Microsoft check, you simply need to change a registry key and restart the PC to "get" the OK to upgrade.

 WINDOWS 11 FOR SENIOR

As you can see, it is a matter of changing registry keys, which for non-pro users could be risky and compromise the proper functioning of the PC.

Email me if you want more information (my mail is **lukas.worley@gmail.com**)

1.3 Installing Using the Installation Assistant

Windows 11, the most recent version, can be downloaded and installed using the Installation Assistant program. First, you'll need to download and run the health check utility to determine whether your computer is compatible. Then, you'll need to download the installation assistant from the website specified below. To download the Windows 11 installation assistant, simply scroll down until you find it and click the "download now" button, as well as we saw just before.

Once the download is complete, you can open the file by selecting it from the list of downloads or by clicking the "open" button if your browser prompts you to do so. The file will be located in the downloads folder on your computer as soon as the utility verifies that your device's hardware is suitable for use.

After that, you'll see a screen that says "**Install Windows 11**". To continue, select "**Accept and Install**". On the licensing terms page, select "Accept and Install."

The installation assistant will then download and install Windows 11. This process may take some time, so please be patient. Once you've completed this step, your computer will automatically restart. Simply click the "**Restart Now**" button. After your computer restarts, the update will automatically install. This process may take some time. Once the installation is complete, please refer to the instructions provided.

 WINDOWS 11 FOR SENIOR

1.4 Run the First Configuration of Windows 11

In this section, we will look at how to perform the initial configuration of Windows 11. This configuration must be done whether you have received a new PC with Windows 11 pre-installed or have upgraded your old PC.

What I will outline are the configuration steps that I perform for my clients or recommend to everyone when I am consulted. Nothing prevents you from making different choices, as these will not affect the operation of your operating system. Let's get started right away.

Step 1

Select your geographic area and choose your keyboard input language. You will be asked if you want to add a second layout or skip this step.

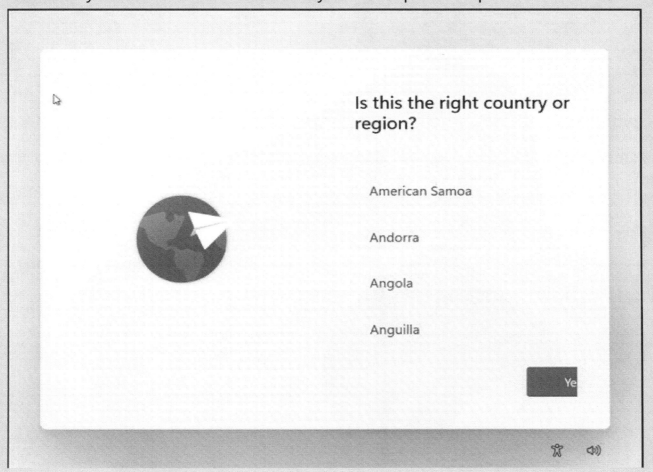

Step 2

At this point, the configuration process will check if you have the latest available version or if any updates are needed. This process is essential to ensure a 100% functioning system.

Step 3

Name your PC and log in with your Microsoft account. If you do not have one at this stage, you can create one.

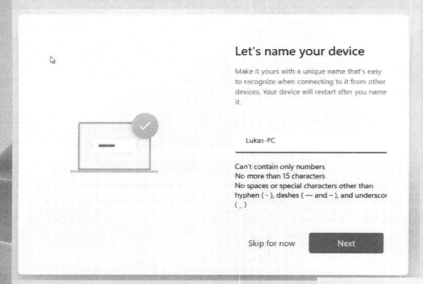

 WINDOWS 11 FOR SENIOR

 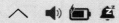

Step 4
Click "Create PIN" to create your PIN, which you will need to log in to your PC.

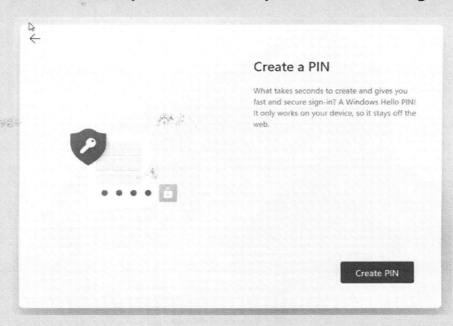

Step 5
This step is about the privacy of your device. Windows will ask for your permission to access the following:

- Your location
- Enabling "Find my device," which is helpful in case of theft or loss of your PC so you can find it again.
- Diagnostic data - Microsoft requires us to collect data so they can improve their service by collecting information about the health of your OS.

These are the main settings, and I usually recommend enabling them. There are also other permissions you can give, and you can decide for yourself how to set them. As I mentioned earlier, these choices will not affect the operation of the operating system (OS).

 WINDOWS 11 FOR SENIOR

Choose privacy settings for your device

Microsoft puts you in control of your privacy. Choose your settings, then select **Accept** to save them. You can change these settings at any time.

Location

Get location-based experiences like directions and weather. Let Windows and apps request your location and allow Microsoft to use your location data to improve location services.

 Yes

Find my device

Learn more   Accept

Step 6

During the initial configuration, Microsoft Windows 11 will ask you what you will use your PC for, such as entertainment, online gaming, work, etc. Depending on your end purposes, Windows will enable or prioritize certain settings over others. The important thing is that you won't have to do anything; Microsoft will handle everything on its own to ensure a 100% functional system for your goals.

Step 7

If you have an Android phone, you can scan the QR code to connect your phone to your PC. This feature was already introduced in Windows 10, but it works very well in Windows 11.

 WINDOWS 11 FOR SENIOR

 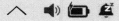

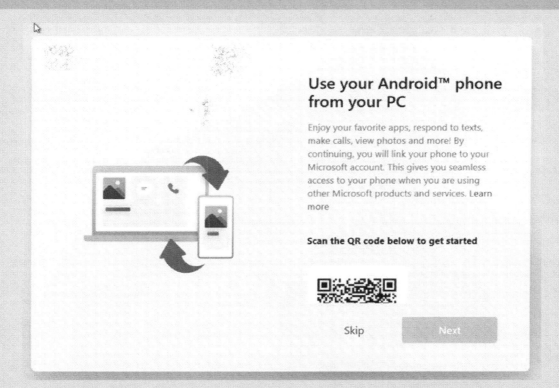

Step 8

If you do not already have a Microsoft 365 package, you will have the option to purchase it during the initial configuration. But why buy something you can get for free (we will see later)? The same can be said for the next step, where you will be asked if you want to have more space in Microsoft's OneDrive cloud.

Step 9

The configuration is finished. As you can see, it was really very easy and fast.

IMPORTANT POINT:

In my case, I was not asked to connect to a Wi-Fi network because I was already connected to the Internet through an Ethernet cable. The configuration procedure immediately recognized this and skipped the Wi-Fi setup. However, if you're using a Wi-Fi connection, one of the first steps will be to connect to one of the wireless networks that the system shows you.

 WINDOWS 11 FOR SENIOR

QUIZ
CHAPTER 1

1 - A trusted platform module (TPM) is a chip that is often attached to:
A) Monitor
B) Keyboard
C) Motherboard

2 - A security feature that prevents malicious software from taking control of your device
A) Secure boot
B) TPM
C) File manager

3 - You will get a message in Windows Update titled when Windows 11 is finally released to the public
A) Get Updates
B) feature update
C) Click here

4 - Microsoft is always working to enhance its products and services, and one of the ways it does this is through.
A) Statistics
B) Analogy
C) Analyzing diagnostic data

 WINDOWS 11 FOR SENIOR

5 - If you are currently using Windows 10 and your device is capable of meeting the criteria, then you should immediately get a notice in
A)   Download area
B)   Files and Folders area
C)   Window Update

6 - How long does the average windows upgrade take ?
A) More than 60 minutes
B) Less than 10 minutes
C) 30 to 60 minutes
D) 15 minutes

7 - What software can you use to make your USB flash drive bootable?
A) Winzip
B) Rufus
C) Windows media player
D) Paint

Answers
1.   C
2.   A
3.   B
4.   C
5.   C
6.   C
7.   B

 WINDOWS 11 FOR SENIOR

CHAPTER 2
CONFIGURING AND CUSTOMIZE WINDOWS

We have successfully installed and configured our new Windows 11 operating system. In this next chapter, we will explore how to customize our system to suit our specific needs, including creating a local account, exploring various methods of logging into Windows 11, and much more. Without further ado, let's dive into this exciting read right away.

2.1 The Settings App

The Settings App in Windows 11 is the central hub where users can manage and customize various aspects of their computer, such as display settings, sound, network settings, privacy options, update settings, and much more. It is a modern, streamlined replacement for the traditional Control Panel in Windows. The Settings App is designed to be user-friendly and easy to navigate, with clear categories and subcategories that make it easy to find the specific setting you want to adjust. It is accessible from the Start menu, the taskbar, and the Action Center, making it easy to access no matter where you are in the operating system. The Settings App is an essential tool for customizing and optimizing the Windows 11 experience.

To launch the settings application, click the "start" button first, then pick the "settings" icon from the menu that appears. Your Microsoft Account may be seen in the top-left corner of the screen. You may modify your information, sign-in choices, email accounts, and other settings by clicking on them here. You will then see a search box just below it, which you may use to look for the settings you need.

 WINDOWS 11 FOR SENIOR

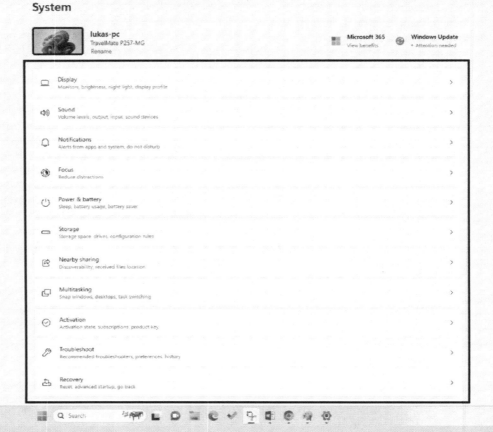

A list of the available categories may be seen along the left-hand side of the page. These are the categories that hold the settings for the many features and choices that are available.

2.2 How to Create a Microsoft Account

A Microsoft account (as well as an Internet connection) is essential to use Windows 11 after its installation. If you are a new user and do not have a windows account, creating one is really simple, just launch your web browser, go to **http://signup.live.com/** and follow the following steps:

- Click the "next" button once you have entered an email address you want to use for your Microsoft Account. After that, you will be prompted to enter a password for the account.
- Remember that passwords must be at least 8 characters long and include a number, a symbol (such as an asterisk, a dollar sign, or a hash), a capital letter, and a lowercase letter. To proceed, click "next."

WINDOWS 11 FOR SENIOR

- After providing your initials and last names in the appropriate sections, choose "next" to continue. The next step is to provide your date of birth and the nation where you reside.
- In the area located at the bottom, please enter the Captcha code.
- Just hit the "next" button. There will be an account established for you. You may now proceed when you have closed the browser window.

2.3 How to Create a Local Account

You may avoid utilizing the Microsoft account by creating a local account on Windows 11, meaning your settings and data will only be visible locally on the device, providing a more secure and private experience overall. Normally, you will want to set up your device with a Microsoft account because it provides additional advantages, such as easy integration with various services and synchronizing files and settings between devices. You can learn more about the benefits of setting up a device with a Microsoft account here. If, on the other hand, you believe that perhaps the other account is not the right fit for you, it is feasible to create a local account that does not connect to the services provided by Microsoft via the Settings screen, Command Prompt, including PowerShell.

The Local User Account for Windows 11

You may avoid utilizing the Microsoft account by creating a local account on Windows 11, meaning your settings and data will only be visible locally on the device, providing a more private and safe experience overall.

 WINDOWS 11 FOR SENIOR

Normally, you will want to set up a device with a Microsoft account because it provides additional advantages, such as easy integration with various services and synchronizing files and settings across devices. You can learn more about the benefits of setting up a device with a Microsoft account here. If, on the other hand, you believe that the other count type is not the right fit for you, it is possible to create a user account that does not connect to the services provided by Microsoft by Command Prompt, including PowerShell.

Follow these steps on the Windows 11 operating system to set up a local account using the Settings app:

To access the Settings menu, open Windows 11.
- Simply choose the Accounts tab and select the tab labeled "**Other Users**".
- Click the Add account button in the section labeled "Other users."

- To indicate that you do not possess this person's sign-in information, use the "I don't have it" option.

 WINDOWS 11 FOR SENIOR

- To add a user who does not have a Microsoft account, choose the option to do so.

Microsoft account

Create a user for this PC

If this account is for a child or teenager, consider selecting **Back** and creating a Microsoft account. When younger family members log in with a Microsoft account, they'll have privacy protections focused on their age.

If you want to use a password, choose something that will be easy for you to remember but hard for others to guess.

Who's going to use this PC?

| User name |

Enter your user name.

Make it secure.

| Enter password |

| Re-enter password |

Next   Back

 WINDOWS 11 FOR SENIOR

- Set up the account recovery questions so you can access your account if you forget your password.
- To proceed, choose the "Next" button.
- After creating the account, select it and then click the icon labeled "Change account type."
- Choose the Administrator account type from the drop-down box next to "Account type."
- To continue, choose the OK button.

After you have finished the processes, the new account will display on Windows 11, and the newbie, depending on the account settings, should be able to sign in as either an ordinary user or an administrator.

2.4 Windows 11 Sign-in option

In Windows 11, you can sign in to your device using various options. The available sign-in options may vary depending on the device's hardware and software configuration. Here are the sign-in options in Windows 11, using "Windows Hello":

1. **Password**: This is the traditional sign-in method where you enter a password to access your device.
2. **Windows Hello Face Recognition**: This method uses your facial features to authenticate your identity (obviously your computer must have a front-facing camera)
3. **Windows Hello Fingerprint Recognition**: This method uses your fingerprint to authenticate your identity (you need a fingerprint reader)
4. **Windows Hello PIN**: You can create a PIN (Personal Identification Number) that is used to sign in to your device. The PIN can be a combination of numbers, letters, and symbols. This is probably the method that is most used by users

You can use the following path to decide the login method:

START > SETTINGS APP > ACCOUNT > SIGN-IN OPTION

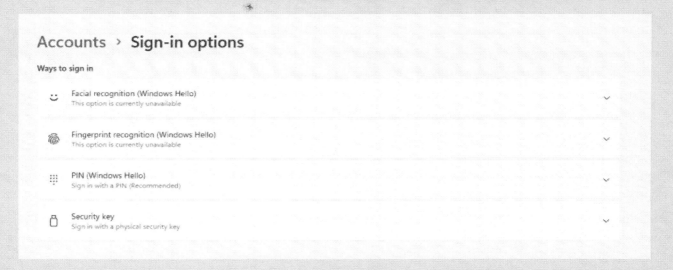

How to change your PIN
- In place of a password, a personal identification number (PIN) may be used to log into Windows:
- Choose "PIN" from the "sign in choices" drop-down menu.
- Select "add" and then "next."
- If you're asked for it, enter the password for your Microsoft account. To change your PIN, type it in now. Please confirm your action by selecting ok.
- Rather than entering your password, you may now sign in using a personal identification number (PIN).

2.5 How to Change Your Account Password
To change your account password, follow these simple steps:

First, access the **Settings App,** then navigate to the **Accounts** menu.

Here, you can manage all your profile settings in a straightforward and intuitive manner, which aligns with the philosophy of Windows 11. For instance, you can set your profile picture, create new profiles with specific permissions, and more.

 WINDOWS 11 FOR SENIOR

 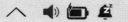

Now, let's focus on the subchapter's topic, which is how to change your account password. Go to the **Sign-in options** menu and at the bottom of the page, click on "**Password**" and then select "**Change your password**".

If you don't see this option, don't worry. If you have enabled Windows Hello sign-in options and are currently signing in using your PIN, you can change your account password exclusively through **account.microsoft.com**.

2.6 Customizing the Start Menu

The fundamental parts of your Windows environment are definitely the Desktop, the Taskbar, and the Start Menu, and for this reason, being able to customize them to best suit our needs is essential. Customizing them in Windows 11 is really very easy, and in the next subchapters, we will see in great detail and specificity how to do it.

2.7 Add Folder to Start Menu

It can be very convenient to add frequently used folders to the "Start Menu" in order to streamline our work. This operation is quick and easy. Simply open the Settings Menu, navigate to Personalization, then select Start and click on Folders. By default, in Windows 11, not all folders are displayed in the Start Menu, so you may encounter a situation like this:

Choose which folders appear on Start next to the Power button.

⚙ Settings		Off ⬤
🗀 File Explorer		Off ⬤
		Off ⬤
		Off ⬤
		Off ⬤
		Off ⬤
		Off ⬤
		Off ⬤
		Off ⬤

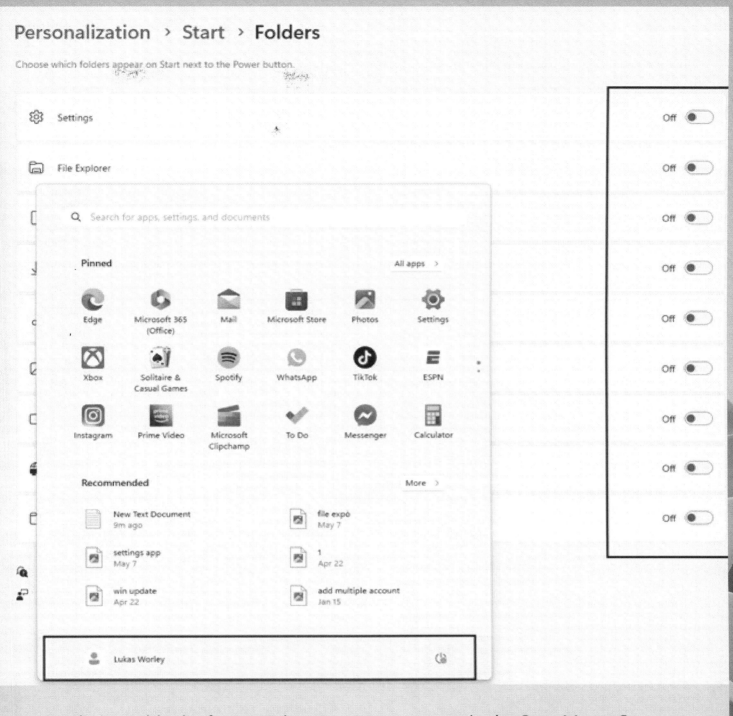

Now let's enable the features that we want to appear in the Start Menu. Suppose we want to display the first four: "Settings," "File Explorer," "Documents," and "Downloads."

 WINDOWS 11 FOR SENIOR

Personalization › Start › **Folders**

Choose which folders appear on Start next to the Power button.

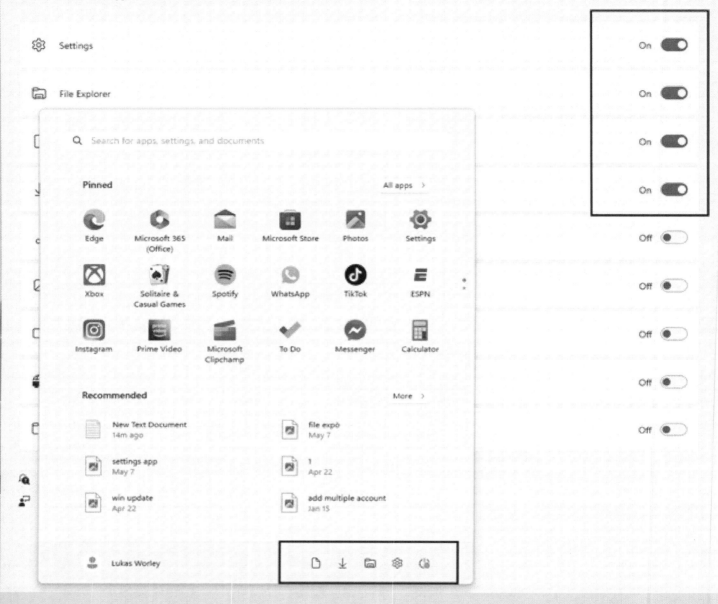

⚙ Settings		On ●
🗀 File Explorer		On ●
		On ●
		On ●
		Off ○
		Off ○
		Off ○
		Off ○
		Off ○

In this way the chosen folders will appear next to the computer's shutdown button.

 WINDOWS 11 FOR SENIOR

2.8 Hide or Show Recommended Items, Most Used and Recently Used App

Start Menu is one of the parts we will use the most, along with File Explorer (which we will see in detail in the next chapter). Customizing it to find the functions we use the most is obviously very useful and will make our lives easier. If we could have a list of all the applications that we most frequently use, our work would benefit enormously. The developers of Windows 11 have thought of just that. It is possible to have a list of the most used apps, the ones we have just installed, and the ones we have recently used. We also have the option to choose which of these to view. To do this, we just need to go to the Settings App-Personalization-Start. From here, we can also change the layout we prefer.

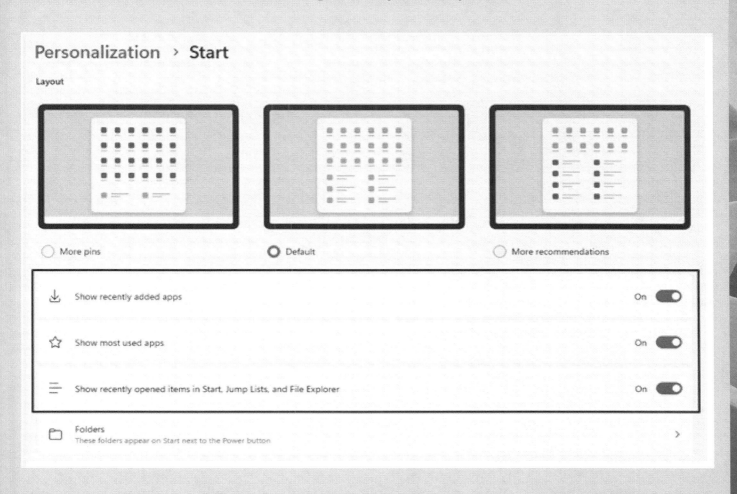

 WINDOWS 11 FOR SENIOR

2.9 Pin and Unpin an App from the Taskbar

After installing and setting up Windows 11 for the first time, the system will have apps pinned by default, but they may not necessarily be the ones you use the most. Let's see how to change this list by pinning and unpinning apps within the Start Menu and Taskbar (the process is the same).

In the next image, we see the default Windows 11 Start Menu, which includes apps that are not of interest to me. Suppose we want to remove Spotify. We can right-click on the Spotify app and select "Unpin from Start." In the case of this app, I see that it is also possible to "Unpin from Taskbar" since I had previously added it to the apps in the taskbar.

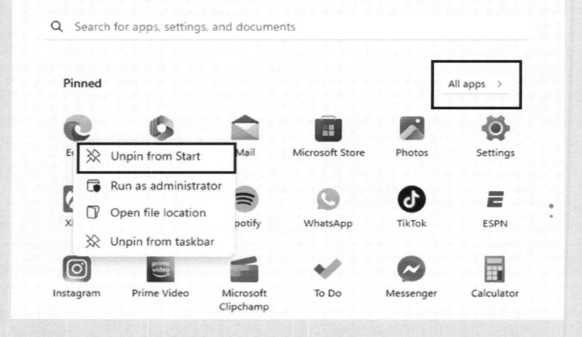

I perform the "Unpin from Start" operation for all apps that are not of interest to me. In the end, I will have a list of only those apps that I am interested in, but which were already included by Microsoft in the list of standard ones.

How do I then add more apps? Where do I find them? It's very simple, just click on the "All Apps" menu at the top right of the Start Menu and we will access the list of all the apps installed on our operating system. At this point, all I have to do is select the app I am interested in and click on it.

 WINDOWS 11 FOR SENIOR

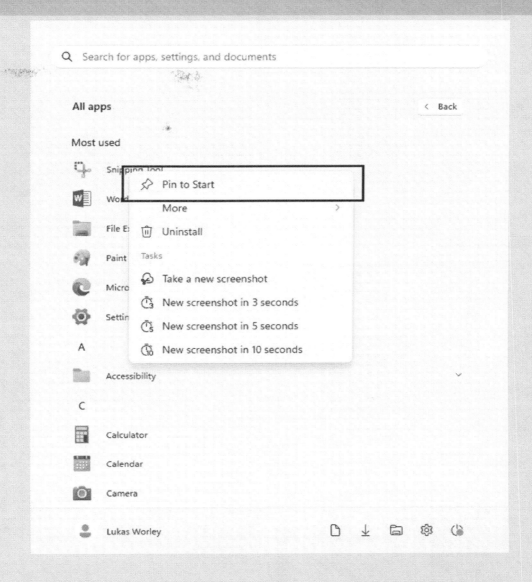

2.10 How to Customize Your Taskbar

First, let's explain what it is: the taskbar is a toolbar usually located at the bottom of the screen that provides quick access to applications and operating system functions. The taskbar can contain a number of elements, such as:

- **The Start button**: provides access to the Windows Start menu, from which you can launch applications, access system settings, and more.
- **Application icons**: provide quick access to open applications or favorite applications that have been added to the taskbar.

- **The notification area**: allows you to display icons of applications that are running in the background and may require the user's attention, such as system notifications, battery and volume icons.
- **The search bar**: allows users to quickly search for files, applications, and content within the operating system or on the Internet.

The taskbar can be customized by the user to suit their needs, such as moving items around, adding new icons of favorite applications, or hiding system icons that are not used.

2.11 Change the Taskbar Color

The level of customization that Windows 11 allows us is really very high. If we want to change the color of the taskbar, we have to go to the Settings app, then to Personalization, and finally to Colors.
To make the change, we have to enable Dark mode (we will see later in detail what it is).

By enabling these modes, it will be possible to choose the color of the taskbar and the Start menu, you will only have to choose the color you want.

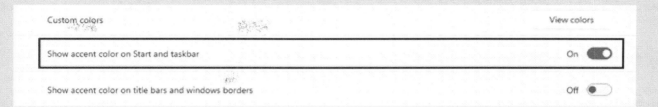

2.12 Change Taskbar Corner

One of the new features introduced in Windows 11 is the taskbar in a centered position, which is almost reminiscent of the taskbar on macOS systems (which are much more visually appealing). However, you can choose to have the taskbar in the traditional left position, just like in all other Windows systems.

To customize the taskbar, go to the **Settings app > Personalization > Taskbar**. In this menu, you have many options for customizing the taskbar. To move all taskbar objects to the left in the "**Taskbar Behaviors**" menu, select "**left**" in the "**alignment**" section.

2.13 Pin App to Taskbar

Having all the apps and folders we use on a daily basis readily available is a goal that every user should strive for, as it enhances their operations. Whenever we open a folder or run a program, its icon appears on the taskbar. If a program is frequently used, it makes more sense to have it already available on the taskbar. To add it, we need to start the program and when its icon appears, right-click on it and select "**Pin to Taskbar**".

In the image below, I will demonstrate how to add Google Chrome to my taskbar:

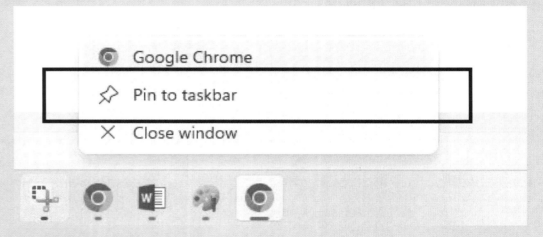

2.14 How to Customize Your Desktop Environment

Let's now shift our focus to personalizing our desktop. We'll explore how to change the wallpaper and select Microsoft's standard icons. In Windows 11, we will only have the "**Recycle Bin**" folder by default, but we can also add the other default folders that were present in Windows 10.

Change the Wallpaper

If we want to change our wallpaper and set a photo of our four-legged friend or a picture with our grandchild (I personally have the photo of my beloved cat on my PC), we can follow these steps: Go to the Settings App, then select Personalization, and finally choose Background.

Here, you'll find a list of all the wallpapers you've recently used, and by simply clicking on any of them, you can set it as your wallpaper.

 WINDOWS 11 FOR SENIOR

If you prefer to import a photo instead, click on "Browse Photo" and choose the image you like from your personal collection.

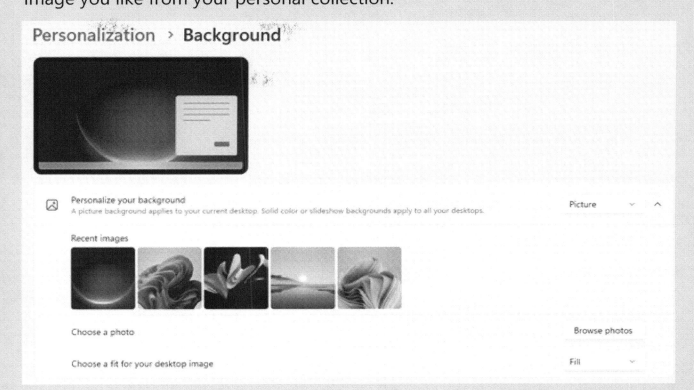

Add Desktop Icon

In Windows 11, the only icon that will be present on the desktop by default after the initial setup is the "Recycle Bin." However, if you prefer to have the four classic folders that were available in previous versions like Windows 10, you can easily restore them.

To do this, follow these steps:

1. Open the Settings app.
2. Go to Personalization and then select Themes.
3. Click on "Desktop Icon Settings," and a window will appear.
4. In the window, you can choose which icons you want to display on the desktop.

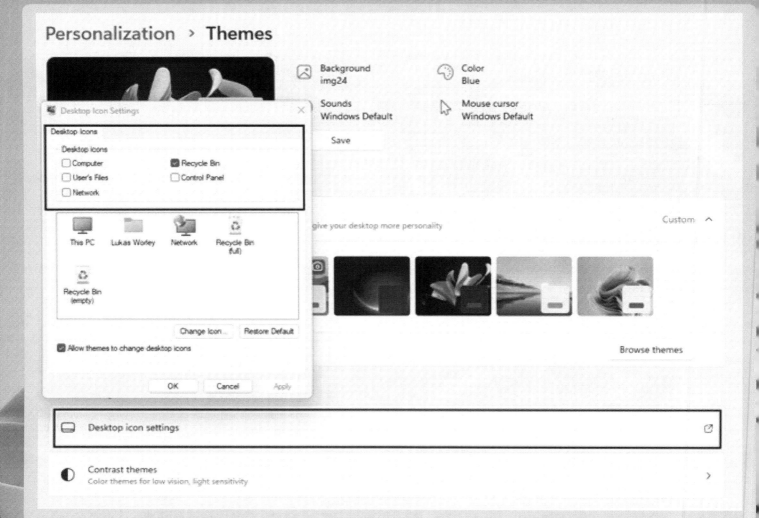

2.15 How to Customize the Lock Screen

The lock screen is the first screen you see when you start up your computer or wake it up from sleep mode and when you lock (**Win + L**) your PC.

It usually displays a background image and some information, such as the time and date, and it may also show notifications. The lock screen is used to prevent unauthorized access to your computer while it's not in use.

 WINDOWS 11 FOR SENIOR

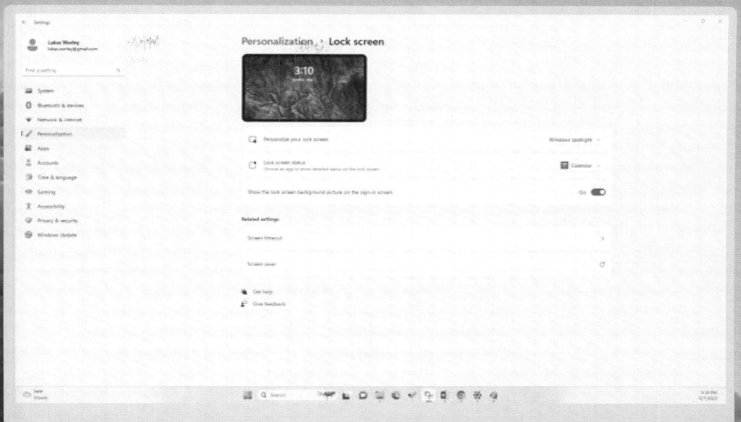

In Windows 11 you have three main options for your Lock Screen.

- **Personalise your screen:** Allows you to choose an image for your background wallpaper on the lock screen.
- **Lock screen status**:
- **Show the lock screen background pictures on the sign-in screen**: By default, the lock screen background picture will show on the sign-in screen

2.16 Dark Mode and Light Mode

Windows 11 offers a choice between Dark Mode and Light Mode (is the default color scheme for Windows 11), which changes the color scheme of the user interface. Here is an explanation of these two modes and what they are used for:

Dark Mode uses dark colors, such as black or dark gray, for the background of the user interface. This makes the user interface easier on the eyes in low-light conditions and can reduce eye strain.

WINDOWS 11 FOR SENIOR

Dark Mode can also help save battery life on devices with OLED or AMOLED displays, as these displays can turn off individual pixels to display true black, which uses less power than displaying other colors.

Light Mode uses light colors, such as white or light gray, for the background of the user interface. This color scheme can be easier to read in bright light conditions, such as when using the device outdoors or in a well-lit room.

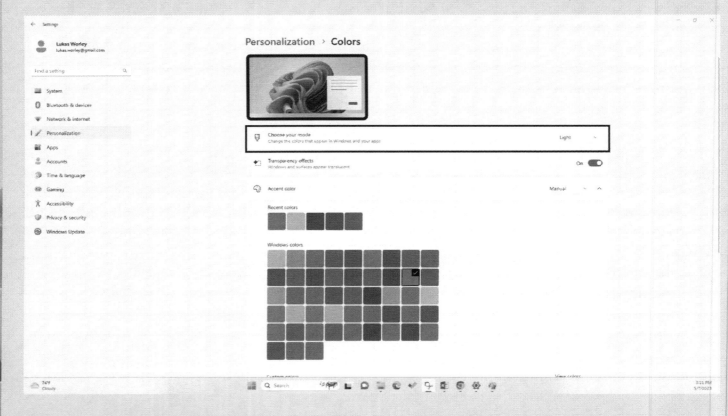

You can switch between Dark Mode and Light Mode in Windows 11, simply follow these steps:

1. Click on the Start menu button in the taskbar and select the "Settings" icon (gear icon).
2. In the Settings window, click on the "Personalization" option.
3. In the left pane, select "Colors".

 WINDOWS 11 FOR SENIOR

4. Under the "Choose your color" section, select either "Dark" or "Light" to switch between the two modes.
5. The user interface will update immediately to reflect the new color scheme.

That's it!

IMPORTANT: some applications may not support Dark Mode so the user interface of these applications may not change when you switch between Dark Mode and Light Mode in Windows 11.

2.17 Windows 11 Themes

In Windows 11, themes are collections of settings that change the appearance of your computer's desktop and windows, such as the background image, colors, sounds and mouse cursor.

Think of themes as a way to personalize your computer and make it look and feel the way you want it to. You can choose from pre-made themes or create your own by customizing individual settings. To get a theme, select a relevant subcategory, click the category's link to see its contents, and then click "Open." The theme will be downloaded to your computer and installed as a desktop background. Alternatively, you can get new themes through the Microsoft Store if you prefer.

2.18 Windows 11 Widget

Widgets are small cards that display dynamic content from favorite apps and services on the Windows desktop. They appear on the widget board, where you can discover, add, remove, arrange, resize, and customize widgets according to your interests. The widgets panel will appear on the left-hand side of your screen. It will showcase a variety of small applets, called widgets, that allow you to perform tasks such as online searching, monitoring the stock market, viewing news and images, and more. You can access the widgets panel by clicking on the widget icon on the taskbar, or you can launch it by pressing the Win + W key combination on your keyboard.

If you are using a touchscreen device, another option is to swipe in from the left side of the screen.

How to Add Widget

To add a widget, click on the panel to open the Widgets panel. Then, click on the "+" symbol to add the widgets you want based on your interests.

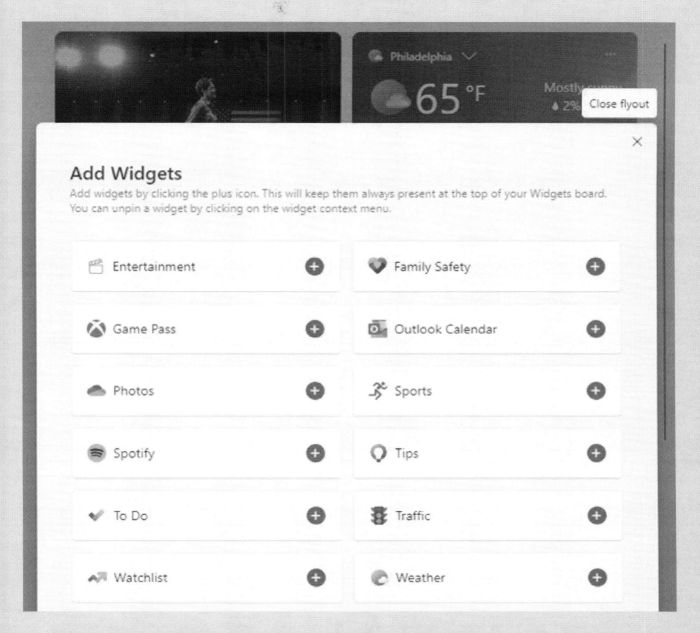

To exit the "widget settings" dialogue box, choose the "x" in the upper right corner of the window.

 WINDOWS 11 FOR SENIOR

Customize Widget

After opening the widgets side panel, select the one you want to customize by clicking on the symbol with three dots next to it. You can modify the size by choosing from small, medium, and large options. To adjust preferences, select the "customize widget" option from the menu. In this section, you can personalize the widget. For example, with the weather app, you can search for your location. The specific configurations available will depend on the widget you are customizing.

Remove Widget

To get rid of a widget, open the side panel for widgets, and then click on the icon that looks like three dots to the widget's upper right. Choose the "remove widget" option.

2.19 Audio and Video Settings

Microsoft Windows 11 offers excellent management of audio and video settings. We can effectively manage multiple output devices by adjusting audio levels individually for each device. All management of video and audio settings is handled as usual through the Setting App:

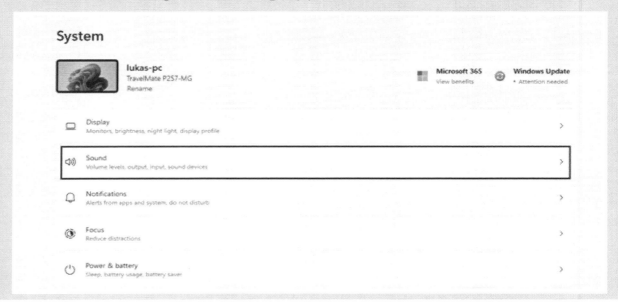

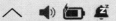

Sound Settings

Audio settings are divided into three sections: Output, Input, and Advanced.

- **Output:**

In this section, we can choose the audio device we want to use. By default, our computer's built-in audio device is selected. However, if we want to use external devices like speakers, we simply need to select the desired device once it is connected.

Within the properties of the output device, we can adjust the volume level, balance, and other settings for the selected device.

- **Input**

On the other hand, this section allows you to manage input devices, such as a microphone. Simply connect the microphone to your computer (ensure that the microphone jack is properly connected).

By accessing the input device settings, you can choose various configurations. You can adjust the sensitivity of your microphone by modifying the input loudness in this section. Additionally, you have the option to change the format, which in turn affects the quality. You can choose between CD quality, DVD quality, or studio quality.

To assess the performance of your microphone, click the "start test" button located in the lower right-hand corner of the screen. As you speak, you will observe the blue bar next to the "input volume" phrase moving. Windows 11 will automatically adjust the input level to match the loudness of the person speaking into the microphone. Once you have finished, click "stop the test."

• Advanced

This section is intended for users with slightly more advanced knowledge, but it is not overly complex. Here, you can access the comprehensive list of input/output devices connected (or integrated) to your computer and manage the Volume Mixer:

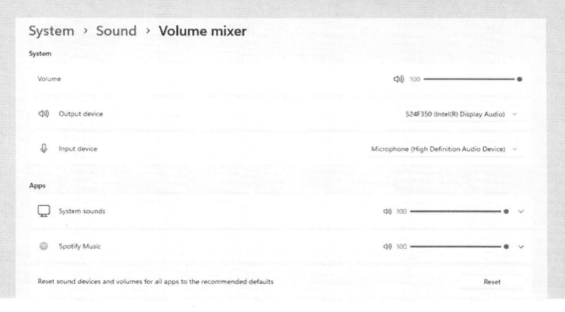

• Volume Mixer

Every program that can generate sound, such as iTunes, web browsers, Spotify, and so on, will have its own volume controls. With this feature, you can adjust the volume for each app individually. For example, you can lower the volume of system sounds while keeping the volume of your music higher, or you can reduce the volume of background music while participating in a video chat.

2.20 Set Date and Time Zone

We will review these settings for informational purposes and to cover the main settings of Windows 11. However, we will not make manual changes to them since they are directly managed by Microsoft if we keep them at their default settings. These settings can be helpful, though, if we accidentally set a different time zone during the initial setup and need to correct it to match our own.

Right-clicking the clock in the lower right corner of the taskbar will bring up the context menu, where you may adjust the date and time. Choose "change date and time" from the list of options.

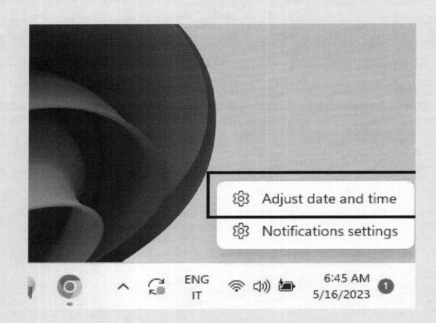

Select the correct time zone for your location here. When Windows establishes an internet connection, it will automatically set the system time. If your location observes daylight saving time, make the necessary adjustments accordingly.

 WINDOWS 11 FOR SENIOR

2.21 Windows 11 Notification

Right-clicking the clock in the lower right corner of the taskbar will bring up the context menu, where you may adjust the date and time. Choose "change date and time" from the list of options. Alternatively, you can open the Settings application and select "System" from the list on the left side of the screen. Then, simply click on the "Notifications" tab.

 WINDOWS 11 FOR SENIOR

In the next section, you will find the option to enable "Show notification banners," which allows the application to display alerts in the lower right corner of the desktop.

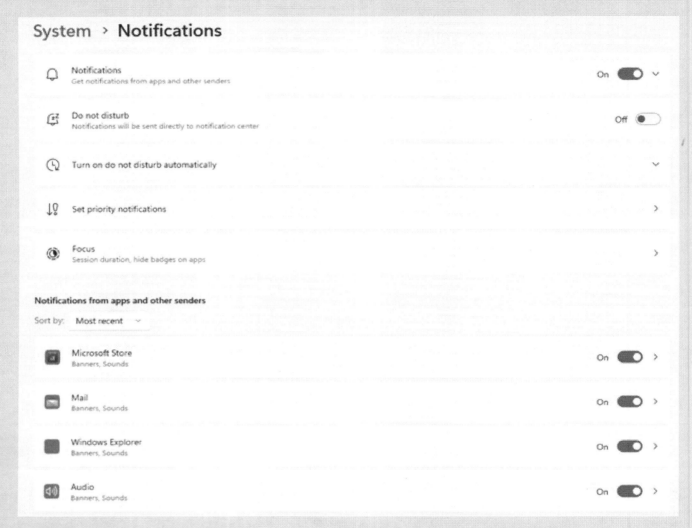

Alternatively, you can choose to display notifications in the notification center. You can also control whether the app's notifications are shown on the lock screen by toggling the corresponding option at the bottom. Additionally, you have the choice to play a sound whenever a notification is received from this application. Simply click on the switch to activate or deactivate the desired function.

 WINDOWS 11 FOR SENIOR

Furthermore, you can customize the priority level for this app. Setting an app's notifications to have top priority ensures that they will always appear first in the list, regardless of the order of other notifications. This can be particularly useful for frequently used applications like reminders, emails, and messages. In the notification center, apps with "normal" visibility are displayed at the bottom of the list, while apps with "high" priority are shown on top of the "normal" ones.

2.22 Power Settings

Windows 11 incorporates intelligent battery management to enhance battery life and longevity. You can access the Power & battery settings by navigating through the Settings App, System, and Power & battery. These settings allow you to have better control over your device's power management. Let's explore them together.

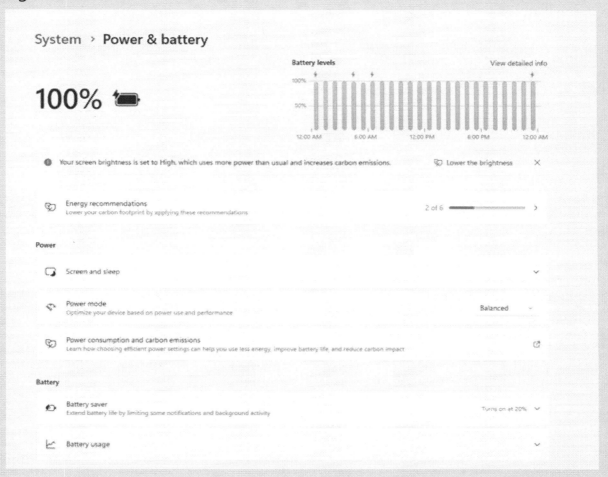

  79

The top section provides us with information about the remaining battery percentage and a graph displaying the battery charge levels over the past 24 hours. By clicking on the details, we can view the specific applications that have consumed the most battery power.

Below that, we have power-saving recommendations. If we delve into the details, we will find all the specific suggestions and can decide whether or not to apply them

System > Power & battery > **Energy recommendations**

Great start—keep going!
Apply energy saving recommendations to lower your carbon footprint
Learn more

Apply all

Set the power mode for best energy efficiency — Apply

Set the screen brightness for best energy efficiency — Apply

Put my device to sleep after 10 minutes — Apply

Turn off my screen after 3 minutes — Apply

Help improve battery by optimizing the content shown and brightness — >

Turn off my screen saver — >

We can also choose how we want to utilize our PC's power, and we are presented with three options: The first option optimizes battery efficiency and lifespan at the cost of performance, the balanced option is a fair compromise, while the third option increases performance at the expense of battery life.
Clearly, the choice depends on our specific needs, but I always recommend leaving it on balanced.

 WINDOWS 11 FOR SENIOR

QUIZ
CHAPTER 2

1 - Rather than entering your password, you may now sign in using a
A)   AppLock
B)   Fingerprint
C)   PIN

2 - You may avoid utilizing the Microsoft account by creating a
A)   Personal Account
B)   Local Account
C)   Admin Account

3 - When Windows establishes a connection to the internet, it will automatically set the system
A)   Zone
B)   Updates
C)   Time

4 - How can you lock your screen?
A)   Unplugging the computer from the electrical outlet
B)   Holding down the pc's shutdown key.
C)   Using the combination Win+L
D)   Using the combination Win+K

 WINDOWS 11 FOR SENIOR

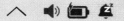

5 - From which modes can you choose the color appearance of the user interface?
A)	Game and user mode
B)	Light and dark mode
C)	Black and white mode

6 - In windows 11, where is the taskbar located?
A)	By default, in the center. But you can move it to the left as in Windows 10
B)	Right
C)	Left

Answers
1.	C
2.	B
3.	C
4.	B
5.	B
6.	A

 WINDOWS 11 FOR SENIOR

CHAPTER 3
WINDOWS FILE EXPLORER

The Windows 11 File Explorer is an application that allows users to view, manage, and organize files and folders on their computer. It is the equivalent of a Finder window on macOS. The File Explorer can be used to navigate through storage drives, search for files, create new folders, copy, move and rename files and folders, and much more. Additionally, with the addition of some features such as quick search and preview display, the File Explorer can make file and folder management much more efficient. In Windows 11, the File Explorer has received an updated graphical interface that includes larger and more modern icons, and a cleaner and streamlined interface.

3.1 What Is Windows File Explorer

The File Explorer can be accessed by clicking on the "Folder" icon on the taskbar or by pressing the Windows key + E on the keyboard (later I will show you all the main keyboard shortcuts). On the main window's left-hand side, you will notice a list containing all the places on your computer where files may be found. The folders and documents you have recently used are shown in the Quick Access list.

 WINDOWS 11 FOR SENIOR

A wide variety of content may be stored in a file, including photographs, movies, papers, spreadsheets, and presentations. A file extension is used to distinguish certain files from others (there will be a dedicated subchapter shortly). The three or four letters following the period are referred to as a file extension, and Windows utilizes these letters to determine the program required to open the file.

Windows Folder Structure

The folder structure in Windows follows a hierarchical organization based on the location of folders relative to other folders and files on the hard drive. Typically, each hard drive has a root folder called "C:" (or another drive letter, depending on how the computer has been configured).

Within the main folder, there are other folders such as "Programs," "Documents," "Downloads," "Music," "Pictures," and so on. These folders are organized logically according to the type of content they contain.

For example, the "Programs" folder contains all programs installed on the computer, while the "Documents" folder contains all documents created by the user. The "Downloads" folder contains all files downloaded from the Web, while the "Music" folder contains all music files.

Folders can be further divided into subfolders and these, in turn, into other subfolders, creating a tree structure. For example, within the "Documents" folder, there might be a subfolder called "Projects," and within "Projects," there might be other subfolders for individual projects.

Folder structure is important because it allows you to easily organize and find files. For example, if you need to find a document, you can go to the "Documents" folder and look for it there. Also, you can create custom folders to organize your files more precisely and tailor it to your needs.

Different Types of Files and How to Use Them

In Windows, like in other operating systems, there are various types of files, the most common of which include:

- Documents: these are generally files created with programs such as Microsoft Word, Google Docs, LibreOffice, etc.
- Images: image files such as JPEG, PNG, GIF, etc.
- Video: video files such as MP4, AVI, WMV, etc.
- Audio: audio files such as MP3, WAV, AAC, etc.
- Archives: compressed files such as ZIP, RAR, etc.
- Programs: executable files such as EXE, MSI, etc.

JPEG, PNG, MP4, ZIP, etc. are named extensions. File extensions are the last three or four letters of a file name, after the period. For example, in a file called "document.docx," the extension is "docx." File extensions indicate the type of file and the program that should be used to open it.

In Microsoft Windows, there are some file extensions that are considered "unknown" or "unsafe" and are blocked by default to avoid possible threats to system security. These extensions include, for example, executables, scripts, and macro files. To open these locked files, you can use the "Unlock File" option in Windows to allow access to the file. However, it is recommended that you use this option only for files that you trust and know the source of, as it may be a security risk to your system to open unknown or unsafe files.

To use these files, you must open the appropriate program to view or edit the contents of the file. For example, to open a Word document, you must open Microsoft Word and use the "Open" function to select the desired file, or an equivalent program (such as LibreOffice or WordPad). To view an image, you can use an image viewer such as Windows Photo Viewer. To listen to an audio file, you can use an audio player such as Windows Media Player. To unzip a compressed file, you can use a program such as Winrar, 7-zip, or Winzip.

How to see the extensions of a file

One objection you might make at this point is, "But I don't see the file extensions, how can I tell?" Don't panic, by default Windows hides file extensions to prevent an inexperienced user from modifying the file extension compromising its proper opening and operation. To enable this feature, open any folder, go to the "**View**" tab, then "**Show**" and enable the option "**File Name Extensions**," and you're done.

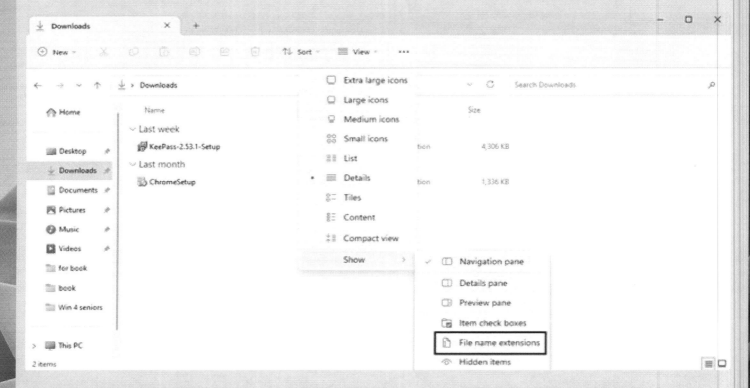

Take care and always be careful not to modify what's to the right of the dot.

3.2 How to Navigate the File Explorer

The Windows 11 File Explorer is organized into many sections, and we will now explore each of them in detail.

 WINDOWS 11 FOR SENIOR

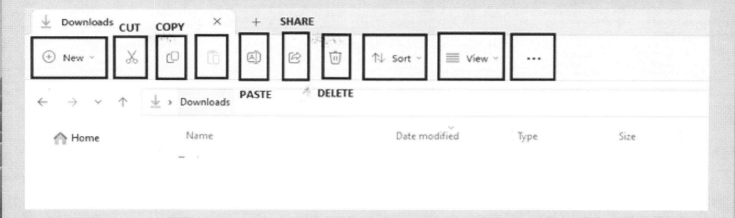

- **New** – If we want to create a new folder, a new text document, a new word file, or a new file in general, just click on "New" and decide which file we need to create.

- **Cut** – is used to move a file from one location to another.

- **Copy** – is used to duplicate a file.

- **Paste** – is used to paste a file that has been previously copied or cut.

- **Share** – in Windows 11, there is a new feature called "Share" that allows you to quickly and easily share files with others, for example, through Teams.

- **Delete** – is used to remove a file from its current location

- **Sort** – It allows you to arrange the files in a specific order of display.

- **View** – It allows you to select the way files are presented, such as using large icons, small icons, list view, details view, etc.

- **More Option (...)** – Clicking on the three dots will open a menu with additional functions, including options like "burn to disk" or viewing the file's properties.

Let us now analyze them one by one with practical examples

 WINDOWS 11 FOR SENIOR

3.3 How to Create and Copy Files or Folders

Creating folders to organize your data is a smart and essential practice. You can have separate folders for papers, work documents, presentations, vacation and holiday photos, college assignments, and more.

Create File

To create a folder, open the File Explorer on your computer. On the left side of the screen, navigate to the desired location where you want to create the folder and click on it. For example, let's say you want to create a folder in the "**Documents**" section.

Next, click the "**New**" button in the toolbar at the top of the screen. A drop-down menu will appear, and from there, select "Folder." You will see a new folder created with the default name "**New Folder**".

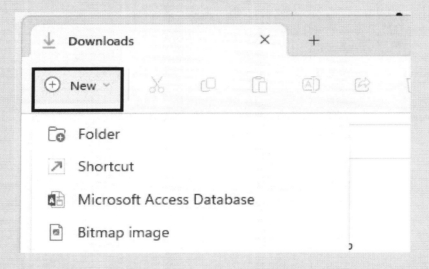

To give it a relevant name, simply delete the text "New Folder" and replace it with a suitable name that represents the collection of documents you will store in this folder.

TIPS: To delete text from a file, you can select it and press the F2 key.

 WINDOWS 11 FOR SENIOR

Copying Files

The process of copying files is similar to that of cutting and pasting. To copy files, open the File Explorer application on your computer.

- Navigate to the folder that contains the file you want to copy by clicking on it in the navigation pane on the left. For example, if you want to copy papers, click on the folder that contains those papers.

- Select the file or files you want to copy by clicking on them. If you want to select multiple files, hold down the Ctrl key while clicking on each file.

- Click the "Copy" option in the toolbar at the top. This will copy the selected file(s) to the clipboard.

- Navigate to the destination folder where you want to paste the copied file(s) using the left-hand pane. For example, you can click on "Documents" and then "Word" to access the desired folder. Use the down arrows to expand folders if necessary.

- Once you have reached the desired folder, click on its name to select it.

- Finally, click the "Paste" option in the toolbar. Windows will then paste the copied file(s) into the selected folder.

Additionally, there are convenient keyboard shortcuts for copying, pasting, and cutting files. These shortcuts will be covered in a dedicated section on keyboard shortcuts later on.

3.4 How to Move Files from One Folder to Another

The process of moving files is similar to using cut and paste. To move files, open File Explorer and follow these steps:

- Click on the folder that contains the file you want to move, such as "book," in the navigation pane on the left.

- Select the file or files you want to move by clicking on them. If you want to select multiple files, hold down the Ctrl key while clicking on each file.

- Choose the "Cut" option from the toolbar menu. This will mark the selected file(s) for moving.

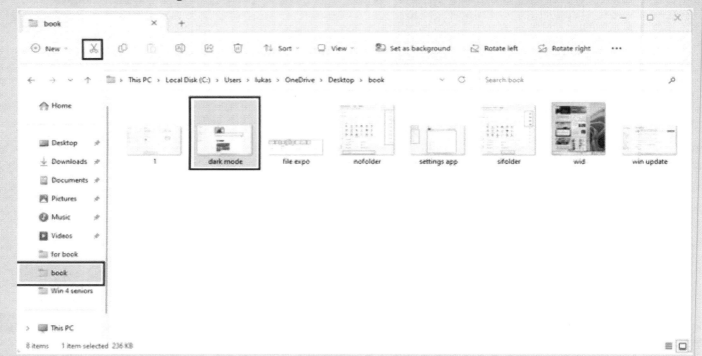

- Navigate to the destination folder where you want to transfer the file(s) using the left-hand pane. For example, you can click on "Documents" and then "Excel" to access the desired folder. Use the small arrows next to the folder titles to expand and view subfolders if needed.

- Click on the name of the destination folder to select it.

- Finally, click the "Paste" option in the toolbar. Windows will move the file(s) and place them inside the selected folder.

 WINDOWS 11 FOR SENIOR

3.5 How to Delete a File or Folder

Deleting files is a straightforward process, and there are multiple methods to delete a file. You can remove files by following these steps:

- Select the files you want to delete in File Explorer by clicking on them. To select multiple files, hold down the Ctrl key while clicking on each file.
- Click the "Delete" button in the toolbar to delete the selected files.
- Another option is to use the Delete key on your keyboard by pressing the DEL key. This will also delete the selected files.

Once files are deleted, they are moved to the Recycle Bin. In a later section of the book, I will provide detailed information about the Windows "Recycle Bin," how it functions, and how you can restore accidentally deleted files from it.

3.6 How to Create a Compressed File

Before we explore how to create a compressed file and extract it, let's first understand what is meant by a Compressed File (also known as an Archive).

A compressed file is a file that has been reduced in size using a compression algorithm. The compression algorithm reduces the amount of storage space required by the file by eliminating redundancies or repetitions of data within the file.

When a file is compressed, its contents are transformed into a more compact form that occupies less storage space. However, in order to access the contents of the compressed file, it needs to be decompressed, or restored to its original form. During the decompression process, the compression algorithm reverses the compression operations, returning the file to its original size and restoring the original data.

To create a compressed file, you need to gather all the files that you want to include in the archive within a folder. Then, you can utilize the native Windows feature to create the compressed file, as depicted in the image:

 WINDOWS 11 FOR SENIOR

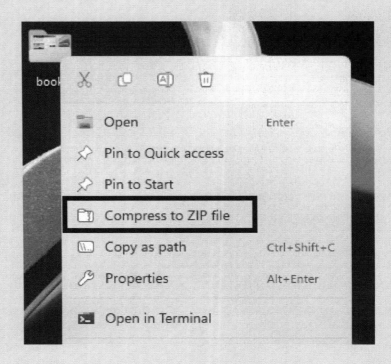

A new compressed file will be created with the same name as the original folder. However, apart from the native Windows software, there are also other free software options available for creating and managing compressed files. Some of the best software for this purpose include:

- Winzip
- Winrar
- 7Zip

These programs offer additional features and capabilities compared to the native Windows software, although the Windows software itself is reliable, albeit with certain limitations.

3.7 How to Extract a Zip File

The process of extracting a compressed file is straightforward, and there are several methods available. Let's explore the simplest ones:

Method 1:
1. Open the ZIP archive that contains the file or directory you want to extract.

2. Drag and drop the specific item or folder you wish to extract to a desired location outside of the archive.

Method 2:
1. Move the compressed file to the location where you want to extract all the files.

2. Right-click on the compressed folder.

3. From the context menu, select "Extract All".

4. Follow the prompted instructions to complete the extraction process.

3.8 How to See the Files or Folders Properties

Getting information about your files is essential as it allows you to identify the file type, creation date, size, name, and make changes such as selecting the application to open it or modifying access permissions. There are two methods to view file properties, let's explore them together:

Method 1:
1. Select the file for which you want to view the properties.

2. Click on the three dots located at the top right of the File Explorer window.

3. From the dropdown menu, select "Properties".

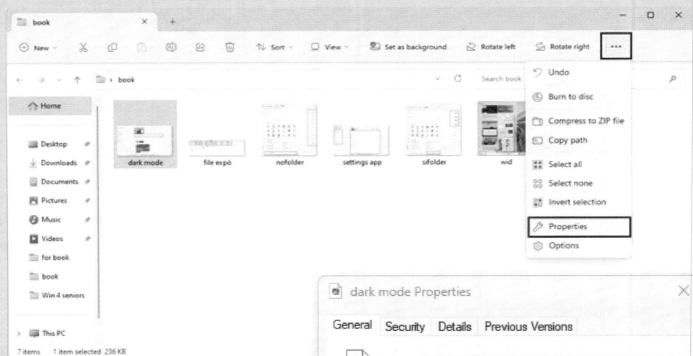

Method 2:

1. Select the file of interest.

2. Right-click on the file.

3. From the context menu choose "**Properties**".

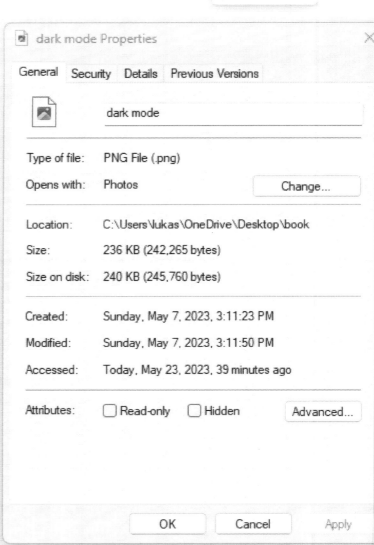

dark mode Properties

General | Security | Details | Previous Versions

dark mode

Type of file: PNG File (.png)

Opens with: Photos   [Change...]

Location: C:\Users\lukas\OneDrive\Desktop\book

Size: 236 KB (242,265 bytes)

Size on disk: 240 KB (245,760 bytes)

Created: Sunday, May 7, 2023, 3:11:23 PM

Modified: Sunday, May 7, 2023, 3:11:50 PM

Accessed: Today, May 23, 2023, 39 minutes ago

Attributes: ☐ Read-only   ☐ Hidden   [Advanced...]

[OK] [Cancel] [Apply]

WINDOWS 11 FOR SENIOR

3.9 How to Use the View and Sort Buttons

In Windows 11, similar to Windows 10, we have the ability to easily choose how to view files within our folders. However, in Windows 11, the management of views is even simpler and more intuitive compared to Windows 10.

You can choose different ways to view files within File Explorer, as illustrated in the image below:

Each type of view may vary depending on the folder you are in. For instance, if you are in the Photos folder, it's recommended to choose "Extra large icons" or "Large icons" as the view.

This allows you to preview the photos and easily select the one you want to view.

On the other hand, if you are in a folder where you store your work files, it would be more practical to use the "List" view.

This provides an organized list of files, making it easier to locate and manage them.

In the "Show" section, you have the option to choose the type of additional panel you want to display, which typically appears on the right-hand side of your File Explorer. You can also decide whether to display file extensions and hidden files.

It is important to be cautious with these settings, as they can have an impact on the proper functioning of your system. Hidden files, for instance, are typically hidden by Windows because they are important for the operation of the operating system.

 WINDOWS 11 FOR SENIOR

Microsoft uses this method as a means of protection to prevent their modification or deletion. Similarly, if you arbitrarily change file extensions, it may compromise the ability to open those files correctly.

Sort

You have the option to arrange files inside File Explorer in various ways, such as alphabetically by name, size, and creation date. File Explorer simplifies the process of finding the specific file you're looking for, especially when dealing with a large number of files in a single folder. To organize your files, select the desired folder from the left side of the File Explorer window.

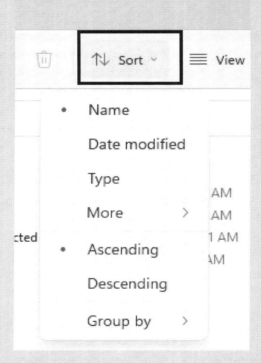

To sort the files, click on "**Sort by**" and then choose the criteria by which you want the files to be sorted. You can sort them based on the date the file was last edited, which will place the most recent files at the top of the list. Alternatively, you can sort them by name, which will display your files alphabetically according to their file names. You also have the option to choose between ascending and descending order, located at the bottom of the menu.

3.10 Undo or Redo an Action

In a later chapter, I will show you all the keyboard shortcuts that can greatly speed up your daily work with the computer. Two of these shortcuts allow you to undo or restore your most recent operation. You only need to press the key combination **Ctrl+Z** to Undo and **Ctrl+Y** to Redo the last action you performed. If you need to undo multiple operations, simply press Ctrl+Z or Ctrl+Y repeatedly.

3.11 Share your Files

Windows 11 introduces an exceptional file sharing feature, which enables you to quickly and easily send files to other devices or individuals. Here's how it works:

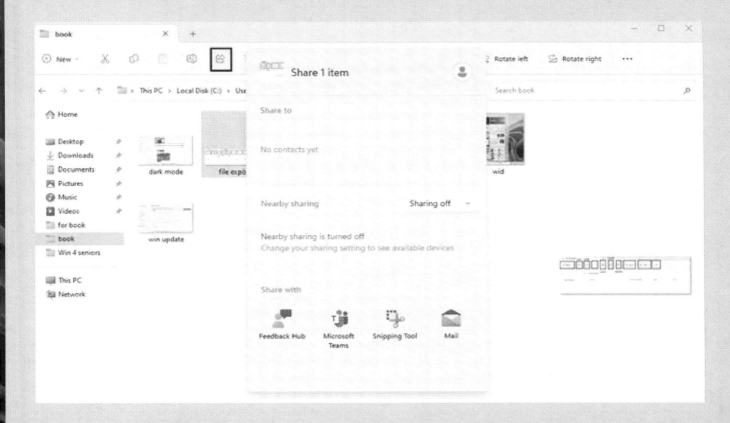

Locate the file you wish to share. This can be any type of file, such as a document, photo, or video. From the File Explorer toolbar, click on the "**Share**" button. The share menu will appear.

The Share pane will display a list of available applications and options for sharing the file. These can include email, messaging apps, social media platforms, or nearby devices.

Choose the desired method of sharing. For instance, if you want to send the file via email, select the email application from the list and follow the instructions to compose and send the email with the attached file. If you prefer to share the file with a nearby device, ensure that both your device and the recipient's device have Bluetooth and Wi-Fi enabled. Then, select the nearby device option and follow the instructions to establish a connection and transfer the file.

Pay Attention: the specific options and available applications for file sharing may vary depending on your device's configuration and the applications installed on your system.

3.12 How to Use Windows Search

You can search for specific files on your computer by using the search bar located in the upper right corner of the File Explorer window. This feature is incredibly convenient as it eliminates the need to remember the exact file location within a folder, requiring only the file name.

Windows will handle the search process for us. To begin searching for a file, first, select the desired starting location, such as "Home."

 WINDOWS 11 FOR SENIOR

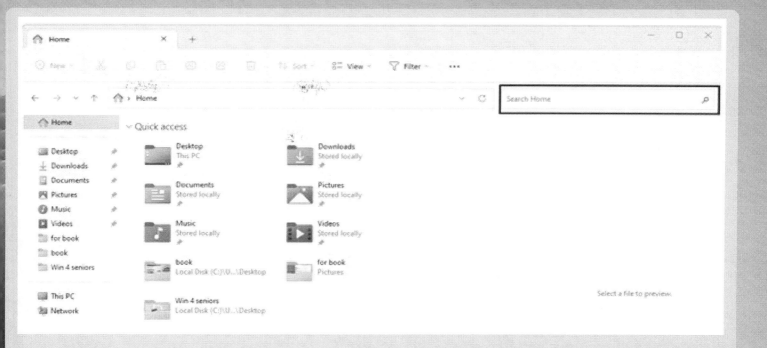

After that, you need to enter your search terms in the corresponding area. A list of suggestions will be displayed, and to select one, simply click on your desired choice from the list. Another option is to utilize the Search Bar located on our taskbar. Here, the search functionality is more extensive as we can not only request Windows to search for files on our PC but also inquire about anything on the web. For instance, if we want to find out the "Weather in New York", we simply need to ask for this information, and Windows will open a web page displaying the relevant details.

 WINDOWS 11 FOR SENIOR

QUIZ
CHAPTER 3

1 - To permanently erase any files that are currently stored in the recycle bin, click the button

A)   Okay
B)   Empty recycle bin
C)   Close bin

2 - If you delete a file in Windows, the file will be sent to the

A)   Recycle Bin
B)   Control Panel
C)   Desktop

3 - What key combination can you use to undo the last operation you did?

A)   Ctrl+Y
B)   Ctrl+M
C)   Ctrl+Z

4 - Which of these are possible image extensions?

A)   JPEG, PNG, GIF
B)   MP3, WAV, AAC
C)   MP4, AVI, WMV

5 - What is meant by a Compressed File

A)   Is a file that similar to original, but degraded

B)   Are the files that are in the recycle bin

C)   Is a file that has been reduced in size using a compression algorithm.

6 - Which of the following is not a file view type?

A)   List

B)   Large icons

C)   Extended

Answers

1.   B
2.   A
3.   C
4.   A
5.   C
6.   C

 WINDOWS 11 FOR SENIOR

CHAPTER 4
CREATE, MODIFY, AND FORMAT A PARTITION

This section is intended for slightly more advanced users, as incorrect partition management can result in your operating system malfunctioning and potentially compromising its functionality. I would like this chapter to be purely theoretical, providing you with a solid knowledge base to enhance your understanding and familiarity with certain concepts and operations. **Let's get started.**

A partition on a Windows 11 PC refers to a dedicated section of the hard disk where data can be stored. The operating system, user data, and any necessary backups are all stored within this volume or virtual sector. Each partition acts as a separate storage area, typically assigned a different drive letter for easy identification (with the default being the letter C). Now, let's explore the various options for creating a partition in Windows 11. You can quickly and easily create a volume using Disk Management, or alternatively, you can utilize the Command Prompt. Take a look at your options and choose the method that appears most straightforward to you.

4.1 How to Create a Partition

To create on a hard drive, you need to be signed in as an administrator, and there has to be either one unallocated disk space or else blank space inside an expanded partition on the drive (hard). The phrases "partition" and "volume" are sometimes used interchangeably.

 WINDOWS 11 FOR SENIOR

If there is no free space on the drive, you may generate some by shrinking an existing partition, removing a partition, or using a tool not included with the operating system to partition the disk.

To access Computer Management, click the Start button on your keyboard. In the Settings app, type "Disk Management" to access the Disk Management Tool. Here, you can view the partition layout of your hard drive and perform actions such as deleting, expanding, or creating new partitions.

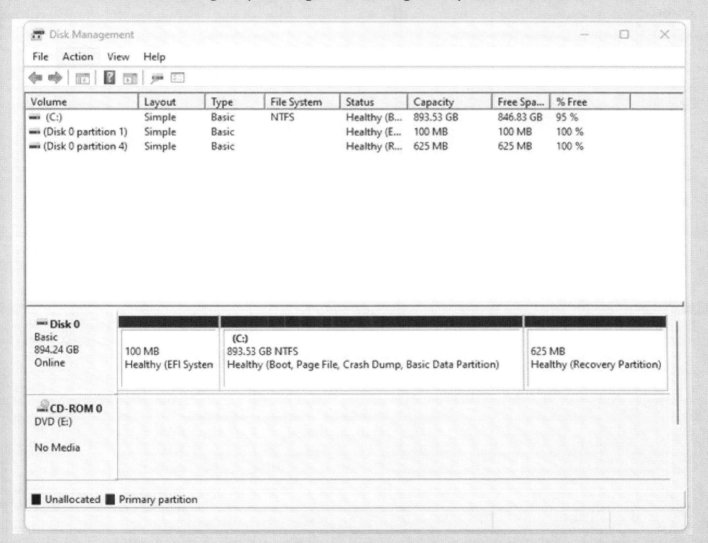

Select "**New Simple Volume**" from the context menu when right-clicking on the unused portion of your hard drive, identified by a black icon indicating it as "**Unallocated**". In the previous image illustrating the disks on my PC, I have no available partitions.

Next, choose the "**Next**" option in the New Simple Volume Wizard. Once you enter the desired volume size in megabytes (MB), click the "Next" button. Alternatively, you can accept the default maximum size. You can either accept the default drive letter assigned or select a different drive letter from the drop-down menu to identify the partition. Then, click the "Next" button.

In the Format Partition dialog box, you have the following options:

- If you don't want to format the volume at this time, select the checkbox labeled "Do not format this volume" and click the "Next" button.
- To format the volume with the default settings, proceed by clicking the "Next" button.

After reviewing your selections, click the "Finish" button.

4.2 How to Expand a Partition

The "**Expand partition**" feature allows you to increase the size of an existing partition by utilizing the available free space on the drive. However, for this to work, the free space must be adjacent to the partition you want to extend, as depicted in the following image. To proceed with the expansion, follow these steps:

- Type "**Computer Management**" in the Windows search box and select the "Run as administrator" option when the result appears.
- In Disk Management, right-click on the partition you wish to expand and select "**Extend Volume**" from the context menu.
- If there is no available free space, but you still want to enlarge the current volume, you can achieve this by deleting another partition. However, this is

 WINDOWS 11 FOR SENIOR

only possible if the volume you want to expand is located immediately after the partition you wish to remove, with no other partitions in between.

- Please note that deleting an existing partition will result in the loss of any data stored on it, so it is crucial to back up your data beforehand.
- Click the "**Next**" button in the Extend Volume Wizard.
- In the next step, specify the desired partition size for expansion or confirm that you are okay with the maximum default size. Any remaining space will still be considered as unallocated, even if the expanded partition doesn't reach the maximum default size.
- Verify that the settings you have configured are correct, and then click "Finish" to complete the volume extension.
- You can locate the expanded partition in Disk Management. If there is any leftover space, it will be shown as unallocated. This unallocated space can be utilized to create another partition if desired.

Remember to exercise caution and ensure you have backups of your data before performing any partition modifications.

4.3 How to Increase and Decrease the Partition Size

To free up allocated space on an existing drive, you can use the "**Shrink Volume**" feature. However, please note that shrinking a partition that contains data may result in data loss. Therefore, it's important to back up any data you wish to save before proceeding with decreasing the partition size.

Follow these steps:

- In Windows, search for "**Computer Management**" and click on the result to open it with administrator privileges.
- Navigate to the "**Disk Management**" section within the Computer Management menu to manage your hard drive.
- Right-click on the disk in Disk Management and select "**Shrink Volume**" to create a new partition.
- The maximum amount of space that can be shrunk will be automatically

calculated, but you can also enter the specific size you want to shrink the partition to. Then, click on "**Shrink**."

- After the shrinking process is complete, you will see a newly created unallocated area in Disk Management. You can utilize this space to create a new partition.

Remember to exercise caution when modifying partitions and ensure you have backups of your important data before making any changes.

4.4 How to Delete or Format a Partition
Here are the steps to delete a partition in Windows 11
:
1. Click on the Start button and type "**Disk Management**" in the search bar.
2. In the Disk Management window, right-click on the disk or partition you want to delete and select "**Delete Volume**."
3. Confirm the deletion by clicking "Yes." This will effectively remove the partition from your Windows 11 disk.

Additionally, you can also delete a partition using Diskpart by following these steps:

1. Press the Windows key and R simultaneously to open the Run dialog. Type "cmd" and press Enter to open the Command Prompt.
2. In the Command Prompt, enter the following instructions one after the other to remove the desired partition.
3. Once you have successfully deleted the partition, you can exit the Command Prompt by typing "exit" and pressing Enter.

Remember to exercise caution when deleting partitions and ensure you **have backups** of **any important data** before proceeding with the deletion.

QUIZ
CHAPTER 4

1 - Expand partition is a feature that enables you to add a room to a/ an:
A)   New Partition
B)   Established Partition
C)   File

2 - With a decreased partition, you may free up already allotted space on
A)   Hard disk
B)   CD ROM
C)   Drive

3 - To quit the Command Prompt, just type exit at the
A)   Prompt
B)   Start
C)   Main menu

4 - To access Computer Management, click the Start button on your
A)   Mouse
B)   Keyboard
C)   Menu

5 - The volume may be created quickly and simply using a disk

A)   Increasing
B)   Management
C)   Decreasing

Answers

1.   B
2.   C
3.   A
4.   B
5.   B

 WINDOWS 11 FOR SENIOR

CHAPTER 5
HOW TO INSTALL AND REMOVE THE APPLICATION

Several media-centric programs are compatible with Windows 11. Whether you have a smartphone or a dedicated digital camera, digital photographs may be organized and improved with the help of a dedicated app. In addition, the software needed to capture pictures with a Windows tablet. Indeed, Windows 11 doesn't natively support playing DVDs. However, third-party software available for download can rectify this situation.

5.1 Installing Apps Via Microsoft Store

The Microsoft Store was formerly known as the Windows Store. It currently sells applications, games, music, movies, and television shows. On your computer's start menu, you should be able to locate the Microsoft Store.

The Microsoft Store has been given a fresh look in Windows 11. You may search for your favorite games, movies, television shows, and applications right here in the app's search area, located along the app's top edge. You'll see a few icons down the left-hand side of the page. You will immediately be taken to the 'home' screen, where you will be presented with a list of suggested applications, popular games, television shows, movies, and so on. When you click on 'apps,' you will be able to look through a wide variety of programs, including those related to productivity, social networking, and photography, as well as tablets and laptops for sale. Choose the "gaming" tab to investigate the most recent games, consoles, gaming PCs, and accessories releases.

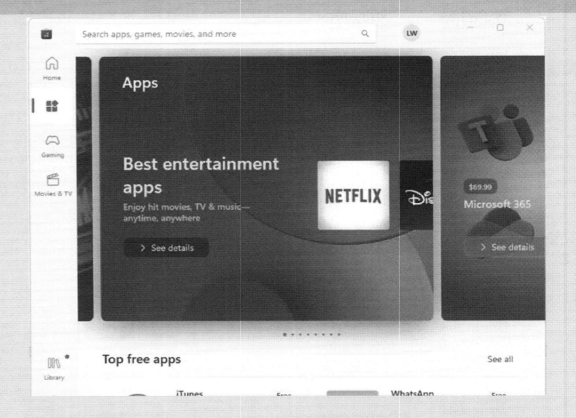

Some applications and games may need money, so you will be prompted to provide your payment information, while others won't cost you a dime. Choose the "entertainment" tab to peruse the most recent releases regarding music albums, television shows, and movies.

You may access your 'library' and 'help' by looking in the screen's bottom left corner. You can discover all of the applications and games you have installed, as well as any movies or television shows you have paid for, in the "library" section of your device.

5.2 How to Install Google Chrome

Chrome, Google's fast and streamlined browser, is a viable substitute for Microsoft's Edge. Installing Google Chrome is really very simple. First we open Edge, the default Windows 11 browser. In the search bar of the browser, type "download chrome" and choose the first search result.

 WINDOWS 11 FOR SENIOR

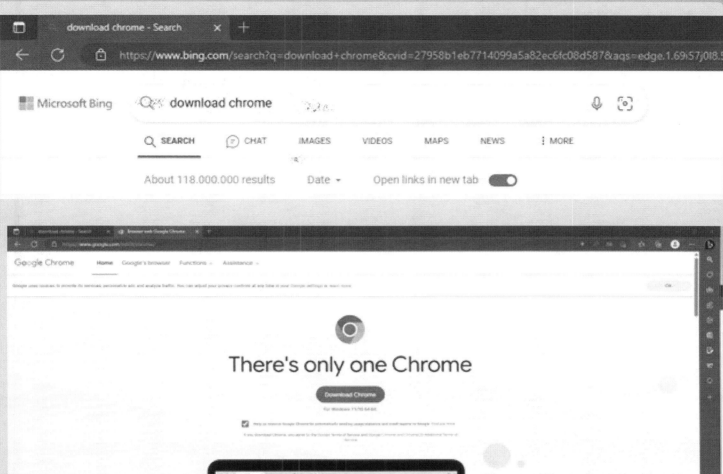

Click on **Download Chrome** to download the executable file and run the **ChromeSetup.exe** file you just downloaded to start the installation process. Follow the steps that will appear on your screen to complete the installation. When the installation is finished Google Chrome will start automatically. But later you will be able to start it by searching from the search bar or directly from the taskbar if you have added it (simply with a click). **Easier than you thought right?**

5.3 How to Install VLC—The Best Media Player

If you want to view DVDs or Blu-rays on your personal computer, you'll need an external DVD drive and a free media player since Windows 11 doesn't come pre-installed with the ability to play them, and newer devices don't come with DVD drives either.

 WINDOWS 11 FOR SENIOR

VLC Media Player is the greatest one I've come across; it can play CDs, DVDs, Blu-rays, and various other file formats.

To install VLC you have two options:

- Installation via the Microsoft Store
- Downloading the executable from the official VLC website

Scenario 1 - Installation via the Microsoft Store

This is the quickest and easiest scenario. In fact, you only need to open the Microsoft Store and in the search bar type VLC.

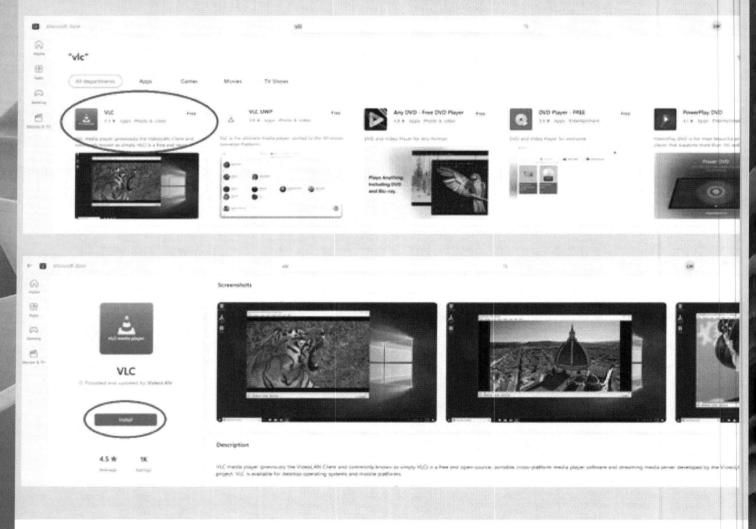

 WINDOWS 11 FOR SENIOR

Scenario 2 - Downloading from the official VLC website

Go to the official VLC website (**https://www.videolan.org/vlc/**) and download VLC for your operating system. VLC is cross-platform software, which means it can be installed on Windows, Linux, Mac, etc. Download the Windows version, which is the one highlighted in the image

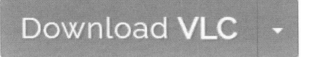

VLC is a free and open source cross-platform multimedia player and framework that plays most multimedia files as well as DVDs, Audio CDs, VCDs, and various streaming protocols.

Download VLC ▾

Version 3.0.18 · Windows 64bit · 40 MB
200,042,231 downloads so far

After downloading the executable file, run it to start the installation. Follow all the steps that are shown to you (they are very simple, always click "**next**" until you get to the end) and VLC will be properly installed on your pc, enjoy.

5.4 How to Install Zoom

Zoom is an online video conferencing and communication platform that enables people to connect and communicate in real time through video, audio, and chat.

It has become particularly popular for business meetings, online classes, virtual events, and personal calls.

Zoom operates through a software application that can be installed on devices such as computers, smartphones, or tablets. Users can create a free or paid Zoom account and then initiate or participate in a meeting or call using an invitation link or access code.

Zoom offers a range of features, including video conferencing, audio calls, chat functionality, and screen sharing. Its user-friendly interface, extensive functionality, and ability to accommodate large groups of participants have contributed to its widespread adoption. It has become an indispensable tool for remote work, online learning, and remote communication.

To install Zoom, you have two options, similar to what we saw for VLC: you can install it through the Microsoft Store or directly from the official website. Let's explore the easiest and quickest method, which is installing it via the Microsoft Store.

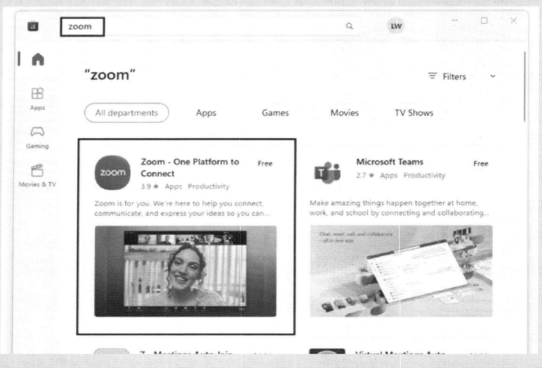

 WINDOWS 11 FOR SENIOR

First, open the Microsoft Store and search for "**Zoom**." The first result that appears should be the software we are looking for. Click on "Zoom" (as shown in the image) and proceed to install the software. Once the installation process is complete, Zoom will be available on your computer. It's that simple!

5.5 How to Install Antivirus AVG

Windows 11 (as well as all its predecessors) natively has an antivirus, Microsoft Defender. Personally, I don't love this solution; I find it less secure than others freely available online. In this subchapter we will look at one of the simplest and safest antivirus that are freely available online, AVG Antivirus.

First we open our browser and in the search bar (if you go to chapter 7 I will explain exactly what the address search bar is and all the components of your browsers), type AVG antivirus download and click on the first result you find:

The AVG executable will be downloaded automatically, and all you need to do is run it to initiate the installation process.

Click on the "Install" button to start the installation process. During the installation, AVG will also provide you with the option to install its browser, called AVG Secure Browser, for free. However, personally, when I install AVG on my clients' computers, I choose to deselect this option as I do not prefer this browser. It doesn't offer significant advantages over other browsers. Once the installation process is complete, your pc will now be protected by AVG.

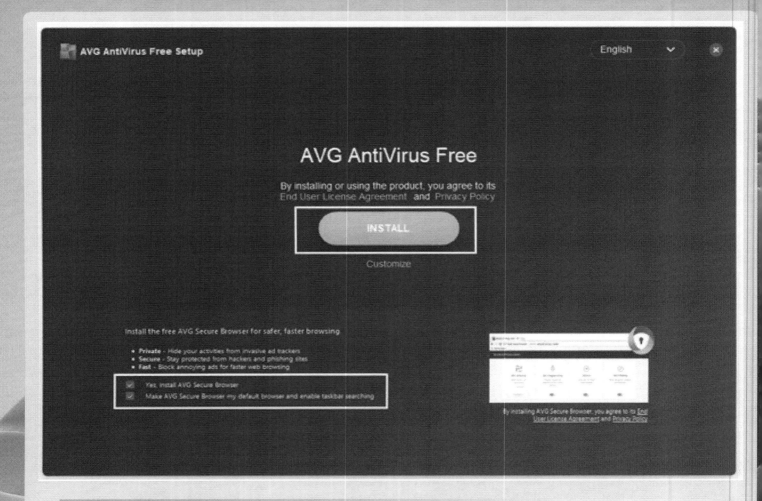

5.6 How to Download and Install any Software

So far, we have covered the installation process for some of the programs that I frequently install on my own computer, as well as on the PCs of my friends and clients. However, the goal of this book is to guide you through the installation of any software you desire or require. In this subchapter, I will explain the different steps you need to follow in order to install any software on your computer.

First, you need to check if the software you are looking for is available in the **Microsoft Store**.

Why is this the first step? It's simple because you can avoid the hassle of searching for the program on various websites to download it, and you can be confident that the software is safe as it is verified by Microsoft.

 WINDOWS 11 FOR SENIOR

However, if the software you need is not available in the store, then you will have to search the web, find the software, download it, and install it. This process can be more time-consuming and potentially less secure compared to using the store (**That's why it's recommended to utilize the store as the first option whenever possible**). So, open your browser and go to a search engine (I recommend Google). Type in the name of the software you need. Let's say you want to install Notepad++, which is widely regarded as the best text editor for Windows (I highly recommend using it instead of the native Windows Notepad).

On Google, you will find numerous results (the same applies when searching for any software). Now, you may wonder: "Among all the suggested sites, which one should I choose?" My answer is: "Always go for the official one." Opting for the official website ensures a high level of confidence that the software is legitimate and not potentially harmful (although antivirus software can provide additional protection).

We then click on the first result, which takes us to the official Notepad++ website, and proceed to download the latest available version. Once the executable file (with the .exe extension) is downloaded, we run it to initiate the program installation.
By following these steps exactly, you will be able to download and install any program you need.

5.7 Uninstall or Remove Apps and Programs in Windows
We will now see the correct way to remove a program that we have installed, including removing all files that may remain in temporary and hidden folders.

To view all the programs installed on your PC, you can use the Settings app, then simply click on "**Apps**" and then select "**Installed Apps**".

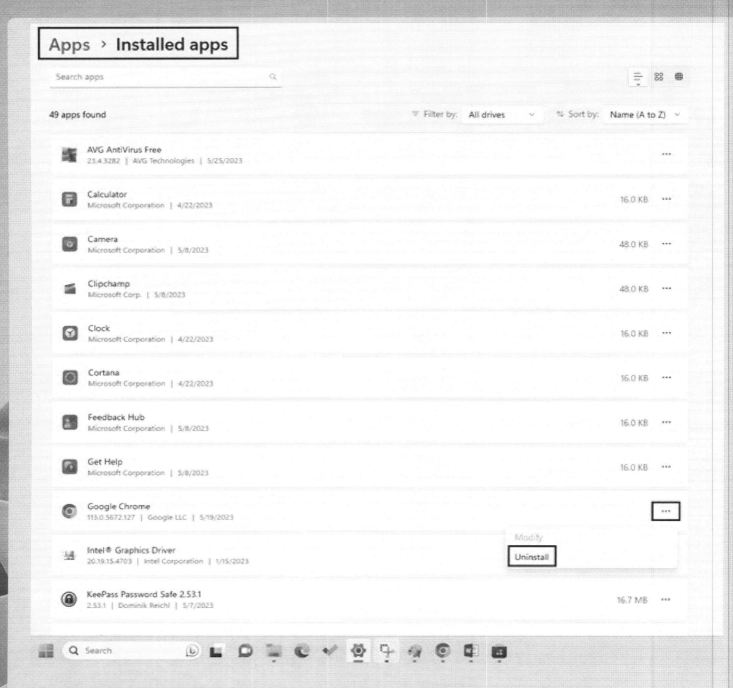

As you can see from the image, all the apps on the computer, whether they are system apps or apps installed by us, are displayed. To remove a program, simply click on the three dots (...) and select "**Uninstall**."

This will initiate the software removal process, and you just need to follow the on-screen instructions.

 WINDOWS 11 FOR SENIOR

Once the process is complete, the software will no longer be present on your PC. However, some files may still remain on the computer, occupying unnecessary disk space. It is recommended to perform a deep clean to remove any leftover files. In chapter 14.7, I will introduce a great program for this purpose.

5.8 Recycle Bin

The "**Recycle Bin**" in all Microsoft Windows systems is a special folder where all deleted files or folders are automatically moved and kept until this folder is emptied. To access the Recycle Bin, you can double-click its icon on the desktop or navigate to the "Recycle Bin" folder via File Explorer.

If a file is too large in size, it is directly removed without being moved to the Recycle Bin. Deleting files is a simple process.

You can remove files by selecting them in File Explorer and clicking the Delete button.

To select multiple files at once, hold down the CTRL key on your computer while clicking.

To remove a file or folder in File Explorer, use the "**Delete**" icon on the toolbar or press the DEL key on your keyboard. All removed files will be sent to the Recycle Bin.

To permanently delete files from the Recycle Bin, select the "**Empty the Recycle Bin**" or "**Empty Deleted Items**" option from the Recycle Bin context menu. This action will permanently delete all files in the Recycle Bin, and you will not be able to recover them.

If you want to **permanently** delete a file without moving it to the Recycle Bin, select the file and press the **Shift + Delete** combination. Windows will prompt you to confirm whether you want to delete the file permanently. However, be cautious because once you delete the file permanently, it may be difficult or impossible to recover it.

The introduction of the "Recycle Bin" in Windows was implemented to enable the recovery of accidentally or intentionally deleted files instead of permanently deleting them from the system. In fact, you can always recover a file that has been accidentally deleted. Here's how:

How to recover a deleted folder or file

If you have accidentally deleted a file, simply go to the Recycle Bin folder and click on the "Restore" button.

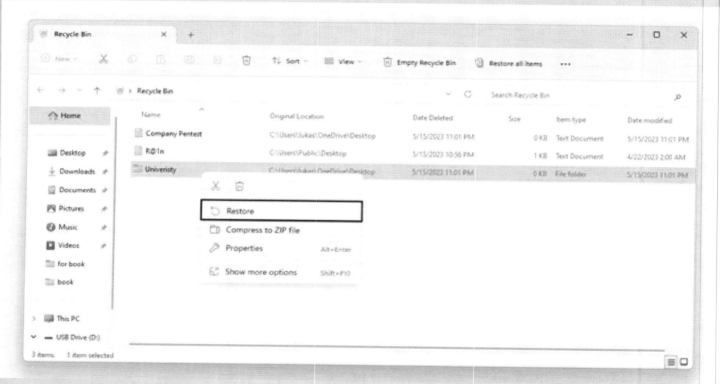

What if you want to recover a file but have already emptied the Recycle Bin?

No need to worry. Thanks to my experience, I will reveal a little-known tip that you won't find in any book on the subject. You can use certain software to scan through the memory space occupied by the deleted file, which is not accessible to users, and attempt to restore it.

However, it is important to note that the chances of success depend on how much time has passed since the file was deleted and whether other files have occupied that memory space.

 WINDOWS 11 FOR SENIOR

The best free software that allows you this is "Tenorshare 4DDiG - Windows Data Recovery"

Go to **https://www.tenorshare.net/**, download and install the last version of this software.

When the software starts, it will ask you where you want to recover the file from, whether it's from the C drive, Recycle Bin, or elsewhere.

Then it will ask you what type of file you want to recover and initiate the scan. Afterward, it will display all the recoverable files, allowing you to choose which one(s) to restore to your computer.

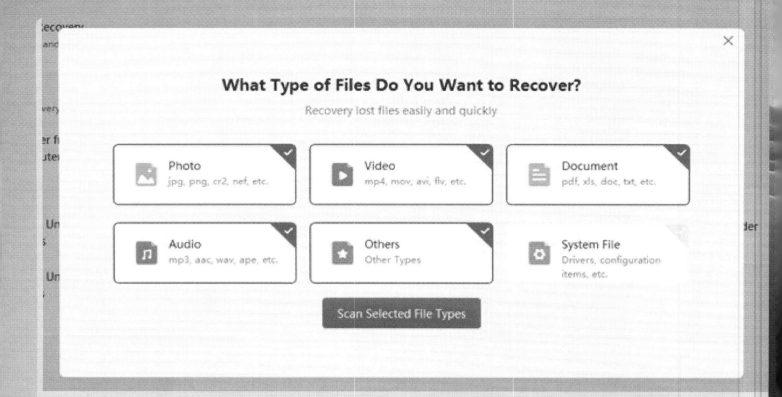

This recovery of deleted files, if a consultant or computer store did it for you, **would cost about $100**.

5.9 How to Use Task Manager

The Windows Task Manager is a built-in tool of the Windows operating system that allows users to view and manage the processes, applications, and services running on their computer.

The Task Manager is used to monitor system performance, identify applications that are using too many resources or are unresponsive, and terminate unwanted or problematic processes or applications. In addition, the Task Manager provides detailed information on system performance, such as CPU, memory, and disk usage.

To access the Task Manager in Windows, you can simultaneously press the "**Ctrl + Shift + Esc**" keys on your keyboard, right-click on the taskbar and select "Task Manager," or press "**Ctrl + Alt + Delete**" and select "**Task Manager**".

 WINDOWS 11 FOR SENIOR

Once the Task Manager is open, users can view running processes in the "**Processes**" tab and terminate unnecessary or non-working processes by right-clicking on the process and selecting "**Terminate Process.**" In addition, on the "Performance" tab, CPU, memory, and disk utilization can be viewed in real-time and in detail.

On the right-hand side of the screen, you'll notice the CPU cores and the graph depicts the activity, showing how much time each core spends carrying out the different activities. You will notice various statistics below, including the uptime, the number of cores and sockets, the size of the cache, the number of processes that are now active, and the clock speed expressed in gigahertz (GHz).

In summary, the Windows Task Manager is a useful tool for monitoring system performance and managing running processes and applications, especially when you want to improve your computer's performance or fix any problem.

WINDOWS 11 FOR SENIOR

QUIZ
CHAPTER 5

1 - To set up your browser, just stick to the prompts
A)   Off-screen
B)   On-screen
C)   Start

2 - How can you uninstall an application?
A)   Click on its icon and delete it
B)   To remove an installed program, you have to go to the Installed Apps, click on the 3 dots and select Uninstall
C)   Format the pc

3 - What is the safest and fastest way to install software?
A)   Microsoft website
B)   Google
C)   Microsoft store

4 - Which provides you with some information on the performance of your CPU, RAM, and hard drives
A)   Start menu
B)   Task manager
C)   Main menu

 WINDOWS 11 FOR SENIOR

5 - If you want to permanently delete a file without moving it to the Recycle Bin, what key combination should you use?

A)   F2 + Ctrl

B)   F4 + Win

C)   Shift + Delete

Answers

1.   B
2.   B
3.   C
4.   B
5.   C

CHAPTER 6
HOW TO USE THE KEYBOARD IN WINDOWS 11

Although a standard keyboard is used in most countries, there are still significant regional variations in layout and language. In this chapter, we will explore how to customize our keyboard to the fullest extent, the available layouts, and the process of changing the keyboard language.

6.1 Customize Touch Keyboard

Windows 11, as mentioned in earlier chapters, was primarily designed with a philosophy focused on mobile devices such as tablets, phones, and touch-enabled PCs. To enhance user text input on these devices, Windows 11 provides a virtual keyboard known as the Touch Keyboard.

All the settings related to the touch keyboard can be found in the Settings App, specifically under the path:

PERSONALIZATION > TOUCH KEYBOARD

You can customize the layout and appearance of the keyboard by selecting a different size and theme.

Choose a theme for touch keyboard, voice typing, emoji and more, and input method editors.

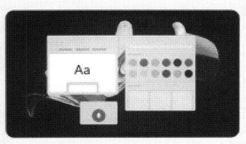 

Theme ⌄

Touch keyboard ⌃

Keyboard size

☑ Show key background

Key text size Small ⌄

View your changes Open keyboard

Related links Show touch keyboard icon in taskbar

As shown in the image, you have the option to change the keyboard size, font size, and even the layout type. You can choose from the default options or unleash your creativity by creating a custom layout.

6.2 Change Keyboard Settings

Altering the keyboard layout is as simple as using the shortcut menu. To access the network and volume settings, use the Quick Settings icon. To make changes to the defaults, open the pop-up window and click the pencil icon in the right-hand corner. Click Edit Quick Settings now to make any necessary adjustments or add to your current collection of frequently used options.

 WINDOWS 11 FOR SENIOR

Now two buttons are visible, including Add and Done, in the Edit Quick Settings box. Next, pick the Keyboard layout from the resulting pop-up menu and click the Done button. Success in adding the Keyboard Layout to the Quick Preferences. After going through the steps above, you can change the keyboard layout under the more accessible preferences. Accessing the Keyboard Layout option has moved to the Quick Settings menu.

6.3 How to Change the main properties of the keyboard

We will now explore how to modify some of the key features of the keyboard, specifically the ones that you will frequently need to change, such as the languages and country of your keyboard. Windows 11 allows you to have multiple languages available for your keyboard simultaneously. To add, remove, or change keyboard languages, follow these steps:

1. Open the Settings App.
2. Go to Time & Language.
3. Select Typing.

Within this section, you will find the main properties related to the keyboard.

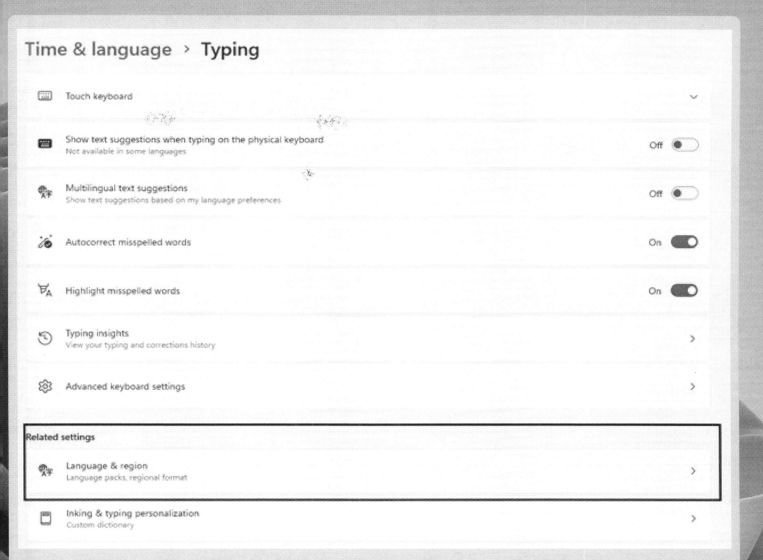

Touch keyboard

Show text suggestions when typing on the physical keyboard
Not available in some languages — Off

Multilingual text suggestions
Show text suggestions based on my language preferences — Off

Autocorrect misspelled words — On

Highlight misspelled words — On

Typing insights
View your typing and corrections history

Advanced keyboard settings

Related settings

Language & region
Language packs, regional format

Inking & typing personalization
Custom dictionary

To change the keyboard language, click on Language & region.
In the Language & region menu, you can modify or add new languages to your keyboard, change the country settings, and import the default language of your Windows 11 operating system.

 WINDOWS 11 FOR SENIOR

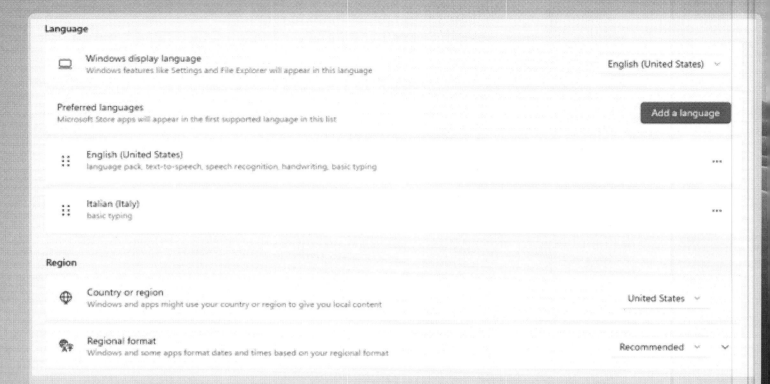

Language

🖵 **Windows display language**
Windows features like Settings and File Explorer will appear in this language

English (United States) ∨

Preferred languages
Microsoft Store apps will appear in the first supported language in this list

[Add a language]

⠿ **English (United States)**
language pack, text-to-speech, speech recognition, handwriting, basic typing

⋯

⠿ **Italian (Italy)**
basic typing

⋯

Region

🌐 **Country or region**
Windows and apps might use your country or region to give you local content

United States ∨

🗺 **Regional format**
Windows and some apps format dates and times based on your regional format

Recommended ∨ ∨

Once you have added the languages, you can easily switch between them using the language menu located at the bottom right corner of your screen.

6.4 Windows keyboard shortcuts

You may not know it, but there is a way to exponentially increase your productivity with Windows. It's not complex, and you don't have to possess hacker or computer expert skills. These are Windows keyboard shortcuts, which are key combinations that allow you to quickly perform certain Windows actions or commands without using the mouse, saving you a lot of time.

For example, suppose you want to copy this text and paste it to a document.

 WINDOWS 11 FOR SENIOR

In the classic mode, you would have to:

1. Select the text you want to copy
2. Position yourself with the mouse over the selected text
3. Right-click and select the copy option
4. Position yourself on the new document where you want to paste the sentence
5. Right-click and select the paste option

A bit cumbersome and slow, isn't it?

You can get the same result in half the time by using shortcuts. In this case, the combination to use would be:

- Ctrl + C to copy
- Ctrl + V to paste

So, all you need to do is:

1. Select the text you want to copy
2. Press Ctrl + C to copy it
3. Position yourself on the new document where you want to paste the sentence and press Ctrl + V to paste

And that's it!

You can use shortcuts for practically anything. You just need to be patient enough to get a little familiar with them and remember the combinations (you can always refer to this book in case you have doubts).

In the next page, I list the shortcuts I use most frequently.

The 16 Most-Used Windows Keyboard Shortcuts

1. Copy selected text - Ctrl + C

2. Paste selected text - Ctrl + C

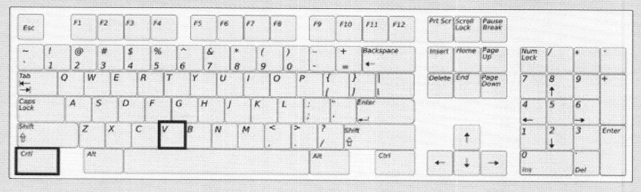

3. Cut selected text - Ctrl + X

 WINDOWS 11 FOR SENIOR

4. Select all text in a document/page - Ctrl + A

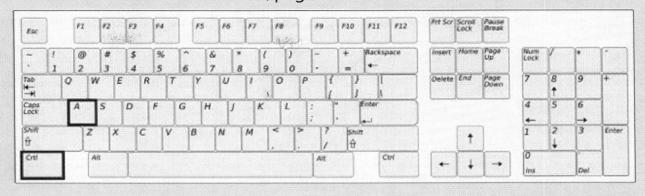

5. Undo the last action you took - Ctrl + Z

6. Restore the last action you took if you had previously undone it - Ctrl + Y

 WINDOWS 11 FOR SENIOR

7. Edit the text using Bold - Ctrl + B

8. Edit the text using Italics - Ctrl + I

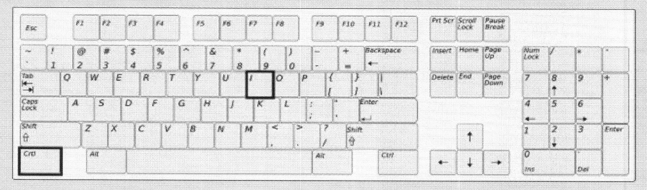

9. Underlines highlighted text - Ctrl + U

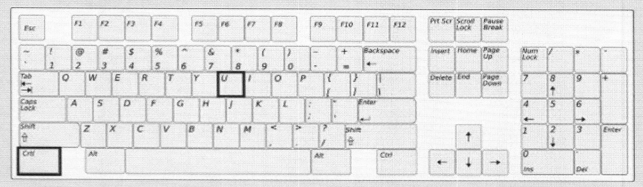

 WINDOWS 11 FOR SENIOR

10.   Opens the Task Manager - Ctrl + Alt + Del

11.   Allows you to switch to another window - ALT + TAB

12.   Closes the current program or application - ALT + F4

13. Opens the Windows file explorer - Windows + E

14. Displays the Desktop - Windows + D

15. Locks the PC and returns you to the login screen - Windows + L

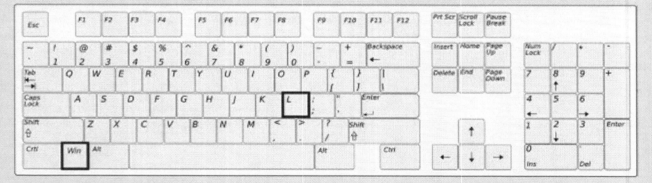

 WINDOWS 11 FOR SENIOR

16.   Opens the Run window - Windows + R

6.5 Function Keys

Function keys are found at the top of all keyboards. On desktop PCs, they can be activated by simply pressing them, while on laptops, you may need to press the FN button + the function key you want to press (e.g. FN + F5). The functions we will see below are standard, but it may happen that some programs have customized the use of individual keys.

- **F1**: The F1 button activates the help function of the program we are using. Sometimes it calls up a section of the program itself, while other times, it opens a web guide or a PDF.
- **F2**: If we select a file or a folder and press the F2 button, it will activate the rename function (which we can also activate from the mouse by right-clicking and selecting "Rename").
- **F3**: The F3 button has the search function and works both within a program and a web page. This is one of the most popular and widely used function buttons.
- **F4**: The F4 function button is one of the least used. Unless there are special destinations, it activates the address bar.
- **F5**: The F5 button is mostly used on browsers (e.g. Google Chrome, Firefox, and Edge) and has the function of refreshing the page. On some sites, such as online newspaper sites, you may need to reload the page to see the latest news, for example.

- **F6**: The F6 button is now used very little. It usually has the pre-purposed function of navigating the address bar of a program without having to use the mouse.
- **F7**: The F7 button activates spell-checking in the Office suite and its free alternatives (such as Open Office).
- **F8**: The F8 button was formerly used to open the temporary startup screen when turning on the computer.
- **F9**: The F9 function button has no particular everyday uses. In some specific software, it has particular functions, but they vary depending on the program.
- **F10**: The F10 button on Firefox and Edge is used to make the menu bar appear/disappear.
- **F11**: The F11 button toggles full-screen mode on or off.
- **F12**: The F12 function button is used to activate the inspection mode on browsers. This is a function used almost exclusively by programmers.

QUIZ
CHAPTER 6

1 - To activate the touch keyboard, launch the
A)   Settings App menu
B)   Main menu
C)   Task manager

2 - A touch keyboard has been introduced to optimize the usability of which devices?
A)   Printers device
B)   Touch-enabled device
C)   Desktop device

3 - Which keyboard key can I use to refresh a web page?
A)   F5
B)   F12
C)   F8

4 - Accessing the Keyboard Layout option has moved to the
A)   Main menu
B)   Quick Settings menu.
C)   Start menu

5 - It's possible to have multiple languages available at the same time?

A)   Yes

B)   No

C)   Only paying for an add-on

6 - Which Keyboard Shortcuts allows you to cut and paste selected text?

     A) Ctrl + C and Ctrl + U

     B) Ctrl + X and ALT + V

     C) Ctrl + X and Ctrl + V

Answers

1.   A

2.   B

3.   A

4.   B

5.   A

6.   C

 WINDOWS 11 FOR SENIOR

CHAPTER 7
INTERNET BROWSING

Internet browsing is the activity of exploring the Internet by using a web browser to access and view content on websites. This activity can include searching for information, viewing images and videos, reading articles, and participating in forums or social media. To do this, we will examine two of the best browsers available to date: Microsoft Edge (the default browser in Windows11) and Google Chrome. I will explain in detail every feature of these two browsers, as well as a few tricks to optimize your work. But first, of course, I'll explain how to connect to the Internet, what modes of connection you can choose, and the advantages and disadvantages of each type of connectivity. So let's get started right away.

7.1 Connect to the Internet—Wi-Fi or Cable

In order to connect to the Internet, you have two methods: Wireless Connection and Ethernet Connection.

Wireless Connection

Each wireless network is identified by a name, which is usually referred to as the SSID (service set identifier), and is protected by a password. You can always change the SSID and password by accessing your modem/router's configuration settings. If you need help doing this, feel free to contact me privately at the email address listed on my site. To find your network's SSID and password, you can check the back of your modem where this information is usually listed.

To connect to your wireless network, you have several options, but we will focus on the easiest one.

Locate accessible wireless networks by tapping the Network/Wi-Fi icon in the system's bottom right corner.

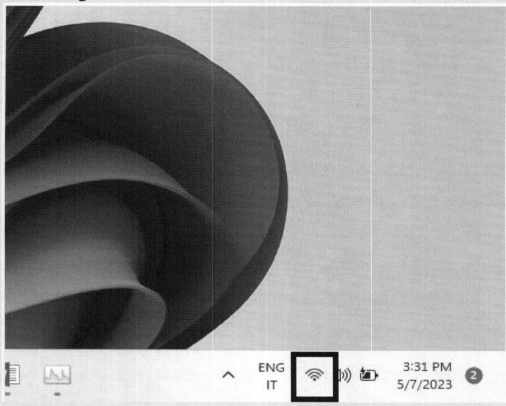

To join a network, choose it from the list, tap the "connect automatically" checkbox, and tap the "connect" button. When prompted, type in the Wi-Fi or network password before clicking "next."

The password or key to your home Wi-Fi network is often displayed on the rear of your router. An SSID is another term for a network's identifier. Follow the same steps if you use a public hotspot at a place like a café, library, hotel, airport, etc. If they have a network key, you'll need to locate it. You may join certain networks since they are public. Remember that most public hotspots do not encrypt the data you transfer over the internet and are unsafe.

 WINDOWS 11 FOR SENIOR

Don't log into your bank account or make purchases over an unsecured network since anybody on the same Wi-Fi network as you might possibly intercept your data.

Ethernet Connection.

To establish an Ethernet connection, an Ethernet cable is required. One end should be plugged into a computer. Don't forget to connect the other side of the wire to your network's router or switch. These days, Ethernet ports are rare in consumer electronics. If so, you can get a USB to Ethernet adaptor. The advantage of a wired network is that it is much faster and more stable than a wireless network. However, it has a major disadvantage due to the length of the cable required. Nowadays, about 90% of connections within home networks are wireless.

7.2 Browsing with Microsoft Edge

Microsoft Edge is the default browser on your operating system and you will find it ready to use. Edge may be accessed from the start menu or the taskbar. The app may be launched by clicking its icon and after launching Edge, you'll arrive at the home screen.

Let's look in detail at all the components of this browser:
1. With this button you can go back to the page you were previously visiting
2. With this button you can move on to the next page
3. With this button you can refresh the page (you get the same result by pressing F5)
4. That's called Address Bar - Here you can enter the URL you want to visit or a search term
5. With this button you can add to your favorites the page you are visiting
6. Pressing this button will take you to the list of your favorite sites

7. With this button you can add the site to your Collection - Use Collections to save content for later
8. With this button you can access your user profile.
9. Clicking on the 3 dots will bring up a menu from which you will have lots options
10. Clicking on this icon you will open the Action Menu Tab.
11. Clicking on the X will close the tab
12. Clicking on the + will open a new tab

7.3 Browsing with Google Chrome

Google Chrome is a viable alternative to Microsoft Edge and, in many ways, offers a quick and streamlined option.
In Chapter 5.2, we saw how it is very simple to install the Chrome software. Now, we will analyze all of its components in detail.

Let's look in detail at all the components of this browser:
1. With this button you can go back to the page you were previously visiting
2. With this button you can move on to the next page
3. With this button you can refresh the page (you get the same result by pressing F5)
4. That's called Address Bar - Here you can enter the URL you want to visit or a search term
5. With this button you can share this page
6. With this button you can add to your bookmark the page you are visiting
7. This button allows you to open the Side Panel – a quick access to your favorites and reading list, web pages that you have previously indicated as interesting.

 WINDOWS 11 FOR SENIOR

8. With this button you can access your user profile.
9. Clicking on the 3 dots will bring up a menu from which you will have lots options
10. Clicking on the X will close the tab
11. Clicking on the + will open a new tab
12. By clicking on this arrow you will be able to see the entire list of tabs you have open on your browser and those you have recently closed

7.4 Set Chrome as Your Default Web Browser

The Chrome Web Browser may be set as the user's default. Here are the necessary steps:

- Access the computer's primary menu by pressing the Start button.
- Select Apps > Settings. Standard Software.
- Chrome may be set as the default browser by clicking "**Set defaults for programs**" and searching for it.
- Click Set default at the top where it says, "**Make Chrome your default browser.**"
- You may leave the settings menu by closing the window.

7.5 What Are Tabs?

Tabs in web browsers are a feature that allows users to open multiple web pages at once within the same browser window. Instead of having to open a new browser window for each page you want to view, you can open a new tab and load the desired page into it. This allows users to quickly switch between pages without having to constantly close and reopen browser windows. Typically, tabs are displayed at the top of the browser window and can be easily managed by, for example, dragging them to change the order or closing them by clicking on the "X" in the tab itself.

Tabs may be seen at the top of a window, and when clicked on, they switch the focus to a new window or tab. After selecting a tab, its contents will be shown, while the other tabs will be hidden. The currently chosen tab is often underlined or emphasized in various colors than the other tabs. The tabs at the front of the interface are meant to look like those on regular file folders when seen from the interior of a filing cabinet.

The following image shows you how to open a new tab: either by clicking on the "+" above the address bar or by right-clicking on the link you want to open and selecting '**Open link in new tab**'.

7.6 How to Add a Bookmark

Bookmarks, also known as 'favorites,' are a feature of web browsers that allow users to save a URL for easy access later. Bookmarks simplify web browsing by allowing users to quickly access a specific website without having to manually type in the full URL every time they want to visit it. Additionally, bookmarks can be organized into custom folders or categories to make managing favorite websites easier.

 WINDOWS 11 FOR SENIOR

Bookmark on Edge

1. Go to the site you want to add to your favorites.
2. In the address bar, you will see a star-shaped button with a "+" symbol next to it.
3. Click on this button to add the web page to your favorites. You will be prompted to enter a name for the favorite and select the specific folder in your favorites where you want to save it.

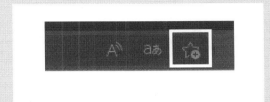

Bookmark on Chrome

1. Go to the site you want to add to your favorites.
2. You will find a star-shaped button in the address bar.
3. Click on this button to add the web page to your favorites. You will be prompted to enter a name for the favorite and select the specific folder in your favorites where you want to save it.

For both browsers, there is a shortcut (using the Ctrl+Shift+N keys) to add a Bookmark

 WINDOWS 11 FOR SENIOR

7.7 How to Show Bookmark Bar

By default, the Bookmarks bar is not visible directly in the browser, but I assure you that it is very convenient to have your favorites list always at your fingertips.

Here's how to enable the Bookmarks bar on your browsers

Show Bookmark on Edge

1. Click on the three dots in the upper right corner to access the settings section and select "**Favorites**".
2. A new tab will open, displaying all the sites you have added to your favorites. You will also have the option to create a folder in your favorites that contains all the sites related to the same topic.

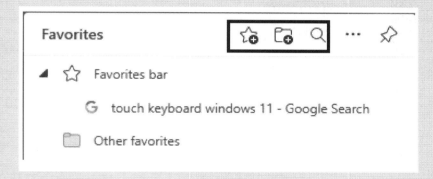

Show Bookmark on Chrome

1. Click on the three dots in the upper right corner, select Bookmarks and then Bookmarks Manager.
2. A new tab will open, displaying all the sites you have added to your favorites. You will also have the option to create a folder in your favorites that contains all the sites related to the same topic.

7.8 Set Your Favorites Home Page

When you open your browser, it is very convenient to have as the first page the website you use most. In my case I love having **www.google.com** as my home page

Home Page on Edge

1. Click on the three dots in the upper right corner to access the **settings** section.
2. Navigate to **Start, Home, and New Tabs.**
3. Click and enable the "**Show home button on the toolbar**" option in the "**Home Button**" menu. Enter the URL you want to set as your home page.

Home Page on Chrome
1. Click on the three dots in the upper right corner and select **Settings**.
2. Go to Appearance and enable the "**Show Home Button**" option.
3. Choose the URL for your home page.

WINDOWS 11 FOR SENIOR

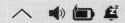

Appearance

Theme
Open Chrome Web Store   ⬈

Show home button   ●━
Custom

○   New Tab page

◉   Enter custom web address

7.9 View Your Browsing History

Whenever you browse a website, your browser stores the pages you visit in a specific location called "Browsing History". As a general rule, it's always a good idea to periodically clean out your browsing history in order to optimize your browser's performance. Let's take a look at how to view and clear our browsing history now.

Browsing History on Edge

1. Click on the three dots in the upper right corner to access the settings section and select "History".
2. A new window will open, displaying all the websites you have visited.
3. To delete a visited site, simply select it and press the "X" that appears to delete it.
4. If you want to delete all the visited sites, click on the three dots to the right of the History window and select "Clear browsing data."

 WINDOWS 11 FOR SENIOR   ⏻

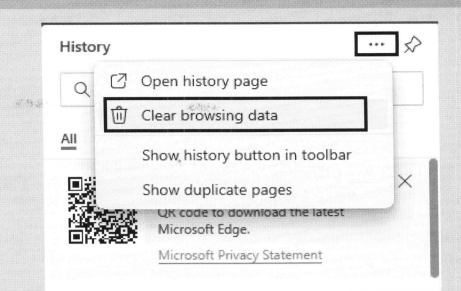

Browsing History on Chrome

1. Click on the three dots in the upper right corner and select History.
2. A new page will open, showing all the websites you have visited.
3. To delete a visited site, simply select it and press the "Delete" button.
4. If you want to delete all the visited sites, click on "Clear browsing data."

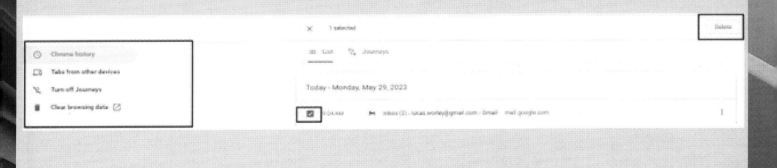

WINDOWS 11 FOR SENIOR

7.10 Browsing in Private Mode

Private Browsing, also known as Incognito Browsing, is a feature found on many web browsers that allows users to browse privately without the browser storing browsing history or saving search data, cookies, or passwords. This feature is very useful for users who want to maintain their privacy while browsing the internet, such as those using a public or shared computer or shopping online without being tracked.

However, **incognito browsing does not guarantee 100% security and privacy**. For example, online activities can still be monitored by your network, internet service provider (ISP), or other parties providing internet services.

In addition, incognito browsing does not hide your online activity from websites you visit or tracking services. These entities may still collect information about your browsing and online activities, even in incognito mode.

Private Browsing on Edge
1. Click on the 3 dots in the upper right to access the settings section and select "New private Windows"
2. A new, darker web page will open that says "InPrivate browsing"

Private Browsing on Chrome
1. Click on the 3 dots at the top right and click on "New Incognito Windows"
2. A new darker web page will open that says "You've gone Incognito"

For both browsers, there is a shortcut (using the Ctrl+Shift+N keys) to open incognito mode.

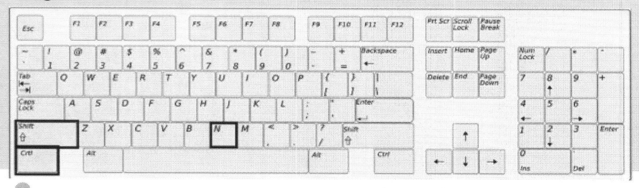

 **WINDOWS 11 FOR SENIOR**

7.11 Install and Manage Extensions

Extensions on browsers are add-on software that users can install to customize and improve the functionality of their web browser. Extensions can add new features to the browser, such as the ability to block advertisements or download videos from websites, or enhance existing features such as password management or incognito browsing.

Extensions can be found and downloaded from the browser's extension store, which is usually built into the browser itself. There are both free and paid extensions available, depending on the functionality they offer. Extensions are available for most web browsers, including Google Chrome, Mozilla Firefox, Safari, Microsoft Edge, and others.

Extensions can be useful for increasing productivity, improving security, customizing the appearance of the browser, and saving time and effort in using the web. However, it is important to choose extensions carefully and only from reputable sources, as some may pose a cybersecurity risk or adversely affect browser performance.

Extensions on Edge

1. Click on the three dots in the upper right corner to access the settings section and select "**Extensions**".
2. Click on "**Manage Extensions.**"
3. A new window will open where you can view all the extensions that are already installed and search for new ones.

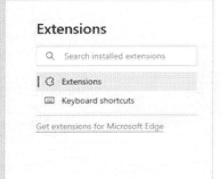
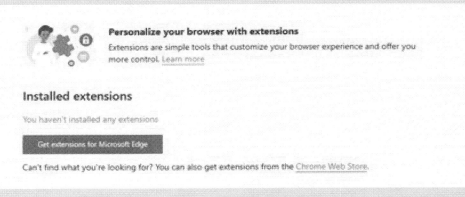

WINDOWS 11 FOR SENIOR

Extensions on Chrome

1. Click on the three dots in the upper right corner and select "**Settings**".
2. Go to the **Extensions** menu.
3. A new window will open where you can view all the extensions that are already installed and search for new ones.

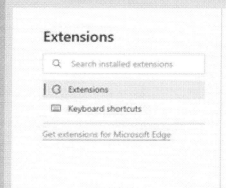
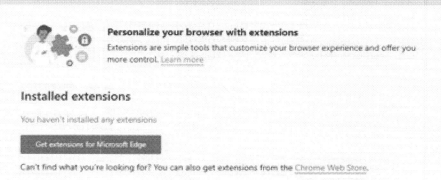

7.12 How to Zoom-in a page

On both Edge and Chrome, it is possible to zoom in on a web page. To do so, simply press the combination of "**CTRL and +**" to zoom in, and "**CTRL and –**" to zoom out.

  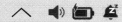

QUIZ CHAPTER 7

1 - Launch Microsoft Edge and enter the ____ you want to save
A)   Web address
B)   Username
C)   PIN

2 - In Windows 11 where is the icon for connecting to WiFi placed?
A)   In the upper right corner of the system.
B)   In the lower right corner of the system.
C)   In the lower left corner of the system.

3 - With which keyboard combination can I add a web page to favorites?
A)   Ctrl + A
B)   Ctrl + D
C)   Win + D

4 - Create a unique name for the
A)   Username
B)   PIN
C)   Bookmark

 WINDOWS 11 FOR SENIOR

5 - In which browsing mode will the websites visited not be stored in the history?

A)   Incognito

B)   Secret

C)   Ordinary

Answers

1.   A
2.   B
3.   B
4.   C
5.   A

 WINDOWS 11 FOR SENIOR

CHAPTER 8
EMAIL WITH FRIENDS AND FAMILY LIKE A PRO

Email is the most convenient method for staying in touch with loved ones worldwide. Communication is just one area where technological advancements have profoundly impacted people's lives in today's online world. We cannot deny that the development of email has greatly facilitated communication between individuals across the globe. However, it has been argued that sending emails, as opposed to handwritten letters, fails to convey the author's emotions. I believe this viewpoint is completely misguided, and here are several reasons why.

It is illogical to assume that an email cannot convey the same level of sincerity as a handwritten letter. While some people argue that the size of a person's words and the spacing between characters can reflect the author's thoughts at that moment, I am confident that how individuals choose their words and express their views is more important than the format or distinctive handwriting when it comes to conveying feelings.

Putting considerable thought and care into selecting the appropriate writing style for an email, for instance, demonstrates professionalism and courtesy and reflects the writer's passion and earnestness for the subject matter.

8.1 Windows 11 Email App

The Mail app is a convenient, user-friendly, and seamlessly integrated email client in Windows 11. It was developed by Microsoft and comes pre-installed with the Windows operating system.

To launch Mail app, click on the Start button, type "**Mail**" in the search bar, and select it from the list of results. Alternatively, you can find it among the "**Pinned**" apps on the Start menu.

If this is your first time using the Mail app, a welcome screen will appear. To get started, click on the "Add Account" button. For previous users of the Mail app, access the "Manage Accounts" menu by clicking on the Settings button located in the bottom navigation bar of the Mail app. From there, select the option to create a new account. Choose the appropriate account type you wish to create, and if necessary, scroll down to view all the buttons in the "**Add an account**" dialogue box.

If you opt to use Google, you will be prompted to sign in, enter your 2-step verification key (if enabled), and grant Windows access to your data. Once you click the "Allow" button, a new account will be established. Please refer to the Special Instructions section for alternative procedures if you are using a different email address. Fill in the required information in the provided fields and click the "Sign in" button. Typically, this will involve entering your email address, login credentials, and account name. Once completed, both the left pane of the Mail app and the Manage Accounts window will display the name of the account.

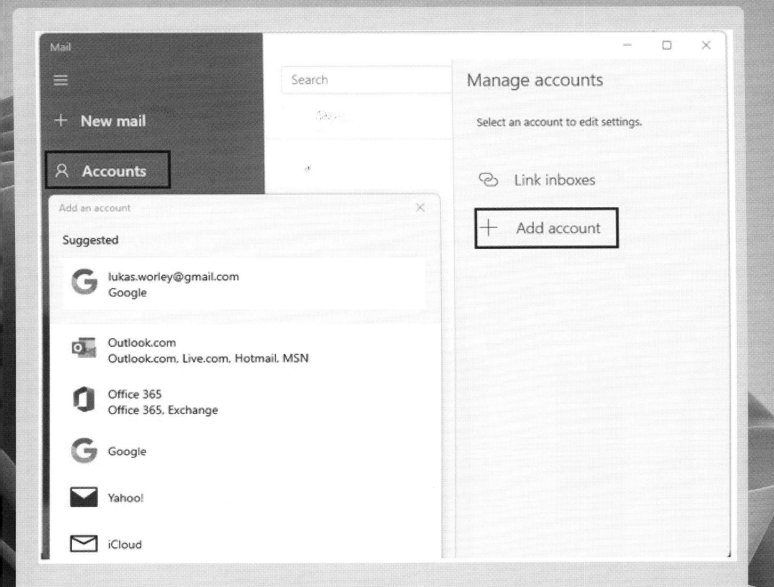

Once you have successfully logged in, your emails will be automatically synchronized in the Mail app, and you can preview them within your inbox folder. In the next section, I will explain how the Mail app works and we will go through the most important features. Let's get started right away.

8.2 Using the Email App

The Windows 11 Mail app is divided into several sections (as depicted in the figure below), which we will thoroughly explore.

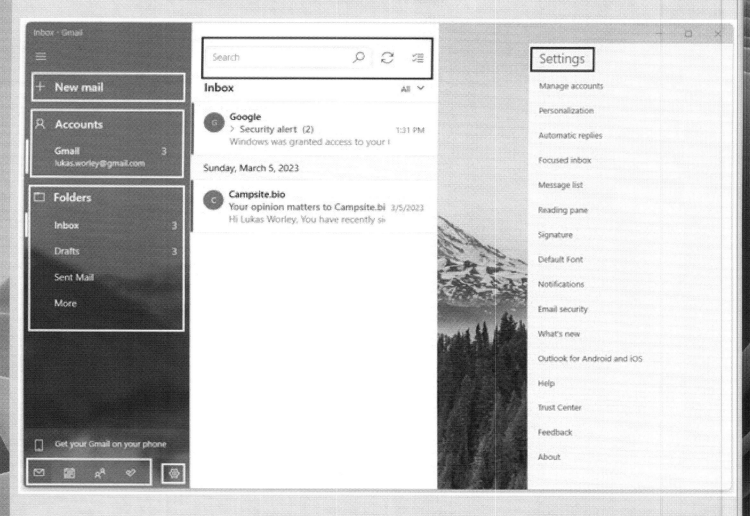

New mail

This section enables you to compose a new email. By clicking on "**New mail**," a new window will open where you can enter the recipient's email address, subject, and the body of the email.

In the "**To**" field, you can also add recipients in the **CC** and **BCC** fields. But what do CC and BCC stand for?

 WINDOWS 11 FOR SENIOR

The CC field stands for "Carbon Copy," referencing the carbon paper used in the past to make copies of a letter while writing it. BCC stands for "Blind Carbon Copy," an extension that allows you to include additional recipients in the email without revealing their email addresses.

Account
Here you have a list of the accounts that are connected to the Mail app. If you have multiple email accounts, you can conveniently manage them all within the Mail app by simply clicking on the desired account.
Later on, I will demonstrate how to add multiple accounts, including my wife Claire's account.

Folders
The "Folders" section displays all your email folders. The default folders include Inbox, Drafts, and Sent items. By clicking on "More," you can access additional folders like Spam, Trash, and others. Later on, we will explore how to organize our folders according to our individual requirements.

Search
It allows you to search for an email by specifying search parameters, such as the sender's name, a portion of the email body, or the subject.

Refresh
Pressing the refresh button will update your inbox to check for any newly arrived emails.

Settings
The Settings section provides options to customize various aspects of your account, such as adding a signature, email protection, fonts, and more.

WINDOWS 11 FOR SENIOR

8.3 Adding Multiple Accounts

People often have multiple email accounts to separate their professional and personal lives. For instance, if you run your own business, you might prefer to use one Gmail account solely for handling client-related emails, while utilizing another account to manage personal finances or other transactions. However, managing two separate accounts can be a hassle and time-consuming. It requires signing out of one account and signing back in every time you want to read or respond to an email.

Instead, thanks to the Mail app, it is incredibly easy to manage multiple email accounts. To add another account, you simply need to follow these steps:

SETTINGS > MANAGE ACCOUNTS > ADD ACCOUNT

Adding another account requires going through the same steps as you did when initially setting up your first account. At this point, in the Account panel, you will see two accounts instead of just one.

PS: Please note that when composing a new message, you should be mindful of selecting the appropriate sender.

8.4 How to compose an email

In section 8.2, we learned how to create a new email by simply clicking on "New Email".

Now let's explore in detail, step by step, how to send a new email using the Windows Mail app. After clicking on "New Email," a new window will open, allowing you to compose your email, specify the sender, and add attachments, among other options.

 WINDOWS 11 FOR SENIOR

At the top bar, we have four menus:

- **Format**: This menu enables us to choose the font, size, style, and color of the text. We can also insert bulleted or numbered lists and apply formatting.
- **Insert**: This menu allows us to add attachments, images, links, tables, and emojis.
- **Draw**: This menu provides options for inserting drawings and other related features.
- **Options**: This menu offers additional functions, such as checking the grammar of our text.

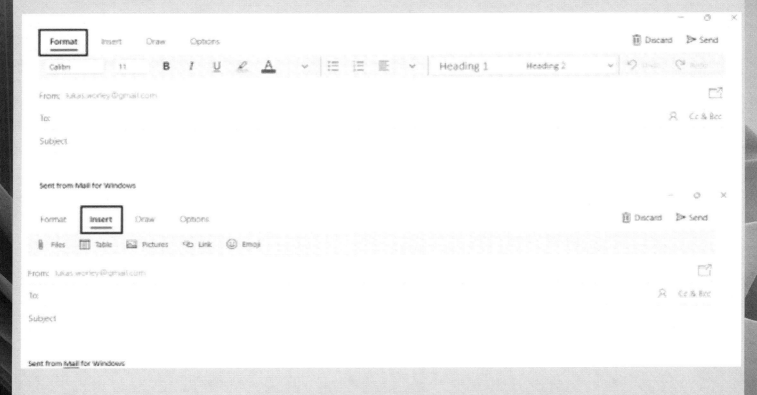

In the "**From**" field, we need to enter the sender of the email. It is usually auto-completed with our own email address.

However, in the case of multiple accounts, we should verify that the sender is the correct one. In the "**To**" field, we will enter the recipient's email address.

 WINDOWS 11 FOR SENIOR

In the "**Subject**" field, we will specify the subject of the email. Lastly, in the body of the email, we can write the desired text.

Once our email is ready, we will click on "**Send**" located in the upper right corner to send it. Now, I'll provide you with an exercise. Please create an email and send it to my email address: **lukas.worley@gmail.com**.

8.5 Read and Respond to Email

With Windows 11, reading and replying to emails is made incredibly easy and efficient, thanks to the Mail app. To read and respond to an email, first, we check if it has arrived by pressing the refresh button mentioned earlier. All received messages can be found in the Inbox folder (or possibly the Spam folder). Then, we open the email that we are interested in reading (simply by selecting it) and wish to reply to.

In the window on the right, we can view all the details of the email, such as the sender, subject, date and time, and of course, the text.

After reading the email, we have several actions we can take:
- **Reply and Reply All**: These options are used to reply to the email. The "Reply" option is used to reply only to the sender of the message, while "Reply All" is used to reply to the sender and all other recipients added in the CC field.

 WINDOWS 11 FOR SENIOR

 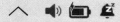

- **Forward**: This option allows us to forward the email message to another email address.
- **Archive**: This action archives the email, storing it for future reference.
- **Delete**: This action deletes the email.

8.6 Organize Your Folder

The folders provided by the Windows Mail App are the default ones. However, every user has different needs and preferences. Now, let's explore how to create custom folders based on our specific requirements and how to move our emails to these folders.

This enables us to maintain an organized and efficient inbox at all times.
Click on the "**Folder**" option to access the full menu. By clicking on the "**+**" symbol, a new field will appear where we can enter the name of the new folder. For instance, if I want to create a folder to organize my students' emails, I can name it "**University**." After typing in the name, I press enter to create the folder. It's a straightforward process, isn't it?

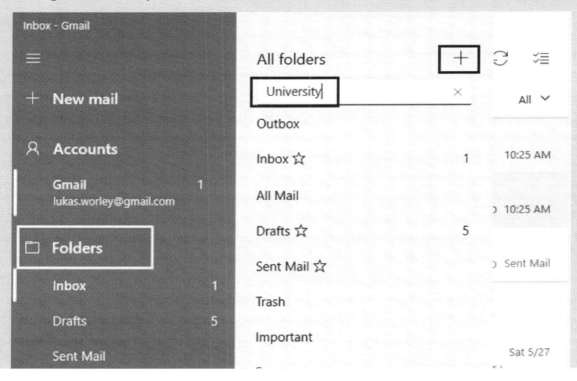

 WINDOWS 11 FOR SENIOR

Now that the folder is created, it is empty. I need to move the emails into it. This process is also quite simple. Just click on the three dots in the top bar, select "Move," and then choose the folder where you want to move the email.

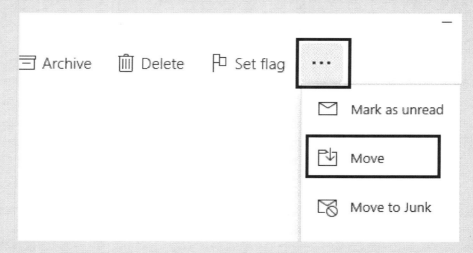

8.7 Spam Folder

One of the significant risks associated with email is the presence of phishing emails and the numerous deceptive emails that we receive daily. Fortunately, all email service providers have systems in place to identify and label such emails as spam. These systems employ complex algorithms that assign a reputation or score ranging from 0 to 10 to each email. If the score exceeds a predefined threshold (determined by the provider), the email is flagged as spam and directed to the SPAM folder instead of the Inbox, providing protection for the user. However, there are instances when legitimate emails are mistakenly marked as spam, while spam emails manage to land in the Inbox. This can occur due to incorrect application of these criteria, resulting in what is referred to as "false positives" in technical terms.

My advice is to never, under any circumstances, open emails that you find in the SPAM folder, as 99% of them are likely to be dangerous emails. It's important to note that emails in the SPAM folder are retained for a period of 30 days before they are automatically deleted by your email provider.

8.8 Google Mail

As far as free email services are concerned, Gmail is undoubtedly the best and boasts over a billion subscribers, making it the most popular choice.
To access your Gmail inbox, you have two options:

- Via Website
- Via Gmail app (currently available only for mobile). Unfortunately, there is no dedicated Gmail client available for Windows 11.

Let's navigate to either **www.google.com/gmail** or **www.gmail.com** and log in to our account by clicking on the "**Sign in**" button located at the top right corner of the webpage. Enter our login credentials to proceed.

Once signed in, you'll notice that the layout and functionality of Gmail are similar to those of Microsoft's Mail App.

At the top of the page, we have the "**Compose**" button (1), which allows us to create a new email.

On the left side of the page (2), we can see the list of **folders**, including the University folder that we had previously created in the Mail App.

This practical example illustrates how the various tools are synchronized between platforms, ensuring that operations performed on one side affect the other.

At the top, there is the email **search bar** (3), and just below that, we find the **list of all our emails** (4).

In the next section, we will explore how to read and respond to emails using Gmail.

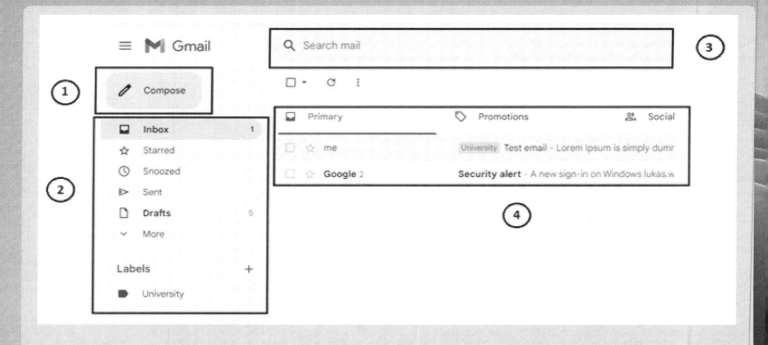

8.9 How to Write, Read and Respond to Email Using Google Mail

If you are already familiar with Microsoft's Mail App, you will have no problem using Gmail right away. To compose an email, simply click on "Compose" and a new window will open in the lower right-hand corner, allowing you to write your email.

Very intuitively, you can enter the recipient, subject, and body of the email. In the lower part, we have various options, let's go through them in order:

- We can change the font, color, format, and size of the text.
- We can add attachments, links, and emojis.
- We can add files directly from our Google Drive.
- We can insert images and add a signature.
- Finally, we have the option to discard the message by clicking on the trash can icon.

Obviously, to send the message, all you have to do is click Send. To read and respond to emails, you can follow the exact same steps we saw together for the Mail App

 WINDOWS 11 FOR SENIOR

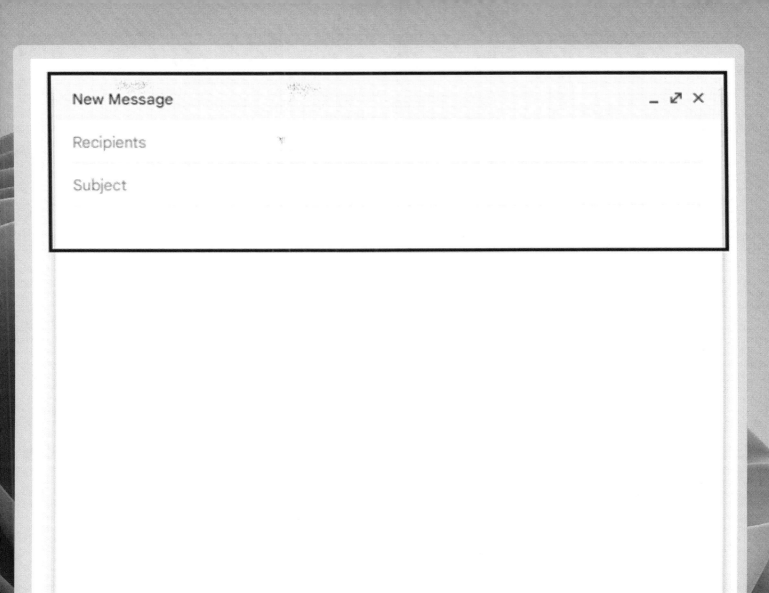

New Message

Recipients

Subject

Send

 WINDOWS 11 FOR SENIOR

 169

8.10 How to know if the recipient read your email?

Now, I'm about to share a little-known trick that can help you determine whether the recipient of your email has opened it or not. Perhaps you've encountered situations where you sent an email, didn't receive a response, and later heard the excuse, "I didn't see it," when you asked why.

Well, starting today, all of that will become a thing of the past. Thanks to this extension, you'll be able to know if the recipient has opened your email by receiving a notification in the form of a green tick mark on the sent email.

The extension in question is called "Email Tracker for Gmail, Mail Merge-Mailtrack." It's free, and no configuration is required. Simply click on "Add to Chrome" to install it. Once installed, click on "Connect with Google" to get started.

Home > Extensions > Email Tracker for Gmail, Mail Merge-Mailtrack

 Email Tracker for Gmail, Mail Merge-Mailtrack
mailtrack.io   Featured

If you want to learn more or encounter any difficulties, feel free to email me, and I'll be more than happy to assist you in setting everything up.

QUIZ
CHAPTER 8

1 - When it comes to free email services, ___ has more than a billion subscribers

A)   Yahoo

B)   Gmail

C)   Hotmail

2 - You may create a new folder by typing a name and then pressing the

A)   Okay key

B)   Yes key

C)   Enter key

3 - An email contained in Spam folder is

A)   impossible to read

B)   automatically deleted after 30 days

C)   reported to the police

4 - To add multiple mail accounts in the Mail App, what should I do?

A)   I have to go to Settings, then manage accounts and add the new account

B)   I need to remove my account and then add the new one

C)   You cannot add more than one account

5 - If you want to add a secondary recipient to your email, in what field should you enter their email?
A)   CD
B)   CC
C)   ACC

Answers
1.   B
2.   C
3.   B
4.   A
5.   B

 WINDOWS 11 FOR SENIOR

CHAPTER 9
INSTALLING DEVICES

One of the main features of Windows 11 is its ability to automatically recognize and connect any device to your computer, allowing you to use it immediately. Unlike other operating systems, such as Linux, where you need to manually download and install drivers for each external hardware device you want to connect to your PC, Windows simplifies this process significantly. That's why Windows is the most widely used operating system among users.

Now, let's explore how to connect major hardware devices to your PC, such as printers, scanners, phones, and more. Let's get started.

9.1 Install Printers and Scanners

As mentioned earlier, device installation on Windows is incredibly easy, as it involves a self-installing process that is completely transparent to the user.

To install a new printer, simply follow these steps:

1. Connect the printer to the computer using the cable provided in the package.
2. Go to Settings > Bluetooth and devices > Printers & scanners.
3. Here, you will see a list of printers that are already installed. Click on "Add Device (1)" to initiate the search for new printers (or scanners).
4. Once the computer detects the printer, simply click on "Add Device (2)" to add the printer.
5. From now on, the printer will be visible in our list whenever we print a document or photo.

 WINDOWS 11 FOR SENIOR

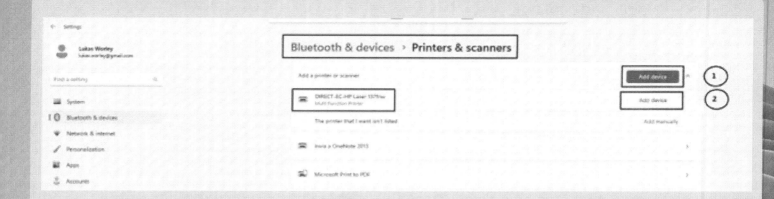

9.2 How to Connect a Smartphone

If you have an iOS device, such as an iPhone, to connect and manage your smartphone, you will need the familiar iTunes or you can make your computer recognize your iPhone as a storage device. This way, you can access it to transfer photos and videos.

However, if you have an Android phone, Windows 11 offers a built-in app called "**Phone Link**" that allows you to manage your phone on your PC.
First, let's launch the app by simply searching for it in the search bar on the toolbar.

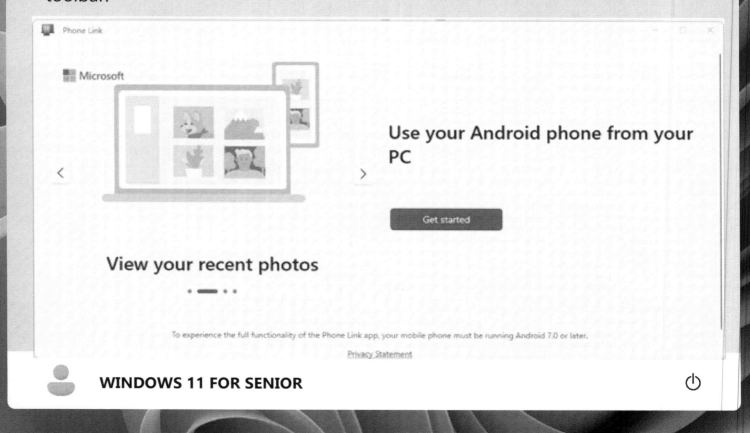

 WINDOWS 11 FOR SENIOR

Then, to initiate the connection between your PC and phone, on your smartphone, navigate to the following web address: www.aka.ms/yourpc and click on continue

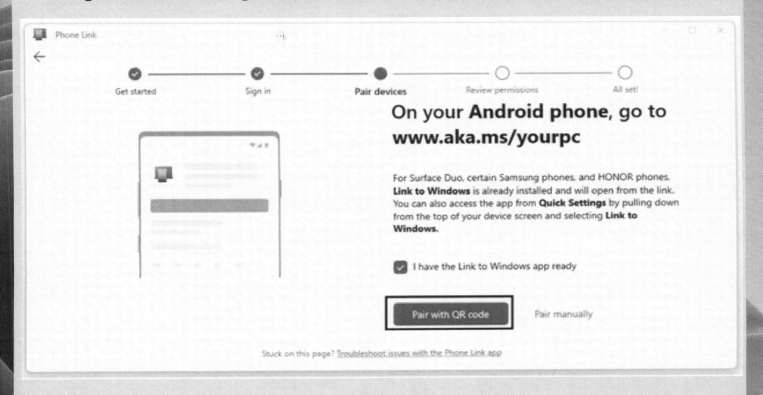

On the computer app, click on "**Pair with QR Code**" to generate a QR code that you will use to pair the two devices.

On your phone, scan the QR code and grant the permissions that are requested. After completing these simple and quick steps, your phone will be connected to the Windows 11 computer. You will be able to read messages, use the apps installed on your phone, view photos, and make calls.

Essentially, **you'll have your phone on your computer**! Isn't that awesome?

 WINDOWS 11 FOR SENIOR

9.3 Mouse Settings

Most computer mice feature two clickable buttons and a scroll wheel, although their designs can vary. Some mice also have additional buttons with customizable functionality. When selecting a mouse, it's important to find one that doesn't cause undue strain on your wrist when using its buttons and scroll wheel. Both wired and wireless mice are available on the market. Wireless mice are convenient as they don't have wires protruding into the user's workspace. These mice require batteries or recharging. Ensure that the mouse comfortably rests in the palm of your hand while in use. You should be able to operate both mouse buttons without discomfort to your wrists, minimizing wrist movement with each mouse click.

On Windows 11, you have the ability to customize certain mouse features, including pointing speed and choosing whether the primary mouse button is the left or right button, among others. You can find all these settings in

Settings > Bluetooth and devices > Mouse

 WINDOWS 11 FOR SENIOR

Bluetooth & devices > Mouse

◻ Primary mouse button   Left ⌄

▷ Mouse pointer speed   ●───────

Scrolling

Roll the mouse wheel to scroll   Multiple lines at a time ⌄

Lines to scroll at a time   ●───────

Scroll inactive windows when hovering over them   On ⬤

9.4 Dual Monitor Setup

When I am at home, one of the most convenient devices I find is definitely the dual monitor. It greatly enhances my work by allowing me to have multiple windows open and accessible simultaneously. Dual screens are especially essential for tasks such as word processing, research, data entry, and accounting. However, I also frequently use them for entertainment purposes, such as playing music on one screen while enjoying a video game on the other.

Let's explore together how to set up and utilize dual monitors:

1. Connect the second monitor to your PC using an HDMI cable.
2. Windows 11 will promptly recognize the new screen, and you should see your screen mirrored on the second monitor.
3. To customize the settings of the second monitor according to your preferences, open the Settings app, navigate to System, and select Display.
4. As you can see, two monitors are detected. By clicking on "**Identify**," you can determine which monitor is designated as the primary and which one is the secondary. To reverse the order, simply select them with the mouse and rearrange their positions.

 WINDOWS 11 FOR SENIOR   ⏻

5. By default, when connecting the second monitor, Windows sets the option "Duplicate these displays," which replicates the same content on both monitors. However, in my opinion, the most useful option is "**Extend these displays**," as it allows you to have one large extended desktop, effectively giving you more screen space.

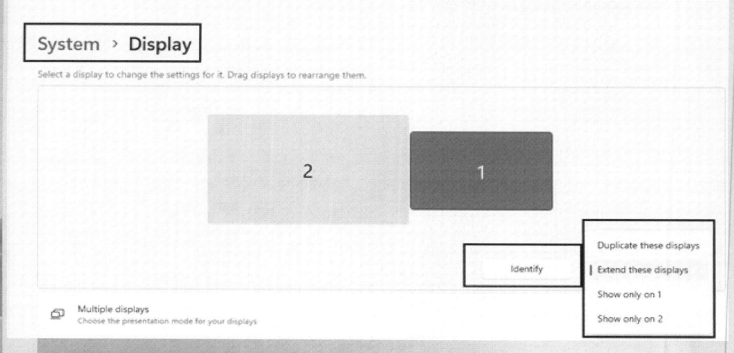

9.5 How to Install USB Devices

Memory sticks, also known as USBs, flash drives, and thumb drives, are the most commonly used portable storage devices. Another option is a portable hard disk. Despite their small size, memory sticks can have storage capacities ranging from 1GB to 256GB. Portable hard disks larger than 1TB are also available.

To use a memory stick or portable hard disk, connect it to a computer's USB port and open the file manager from the system tray. In File Explorer, locate the drive in the "This PC" folder. To expand the view in 'This PC', click on the arrow to the left. You can access the contents of a drive by clicking on its icon. The external hard disk is usually assigned a letter following "C." Usually, we are referring to drive D.

 WINDOWS 11 FOR SENIOR

QUIZ
CHAPTER 9

1 - A memory stick's storage capacity may be anything from
A)   1GB to 256GB
B)   2 GB to 128GB
C)   1 GB to 365GB

2 - ____ mice are convenient since they don't protrude any wires into the user's workspace
A)   Wired
B)   Wireless
C)   Bluetooth

3 - _____ requires a connection between your Android device and Windows to function
A)   Data Link
B)   Wired Link
C)   Phone Link

4 - What do you need to connect a second montitor?
A)   An HDMI cable
B)   An Ethernet cable
C)   A WiFi connection

5 - Which of the following is a dual monitor display option

A)   Dispaly only the main screen
B)   Duplicate these displays
C)   Dispaly only the secondary screen

Answers

1.   A
2.   B
3.   C
4.   A
5.   B

WINDOWS 11 FOR SENIOR

CHAPTER 10
APP AND TIPS FOR DAILY ROUTINE

Microsoft Windows 11 can also be very useful for better organizing our day and keeping track of our commitments, helping us avoid forgetting tasks. It provides us with numerous apps for our daily routine. The Microsoft Store offers a vast selection of apps available for download. You can find a wide variety of apps, including those for gaming, productivity, and even health. Whether you're looking for apps for gaming, media consumption, or serious work in areas like word processing, design, and illustration, the Microsoft Store has you covered. We will now take a closer look at what, in my opinion, are the best apps that we can use on a daily basis.

10.1 Microsoft Teams

Microsoft Teams is a communication and collaboration platform that enables seamless teamwork and productivity. With Teams, you can easily connect with others through video calls, instant messaging, document sharing, and project collaboration. It serves as a virtual hub where you can meet and work together, regardless of geographical distance. Whether it's for business meetings, online learning, or staying connected with friends and colleagues, Teams provides a versatile and efficient platform.

Microsoft Teams has become so popular that it comes pre-installed as a default app in Windows 11, making it readily accessible.

Now, let's explore how to access and customize Teams for your needs.

 WINDOWS 11 FOR SENIOR

In the search bar, type "**Microsoft Teams**" and launch the app. Once it opens, you will need to log in by entering your credentials.

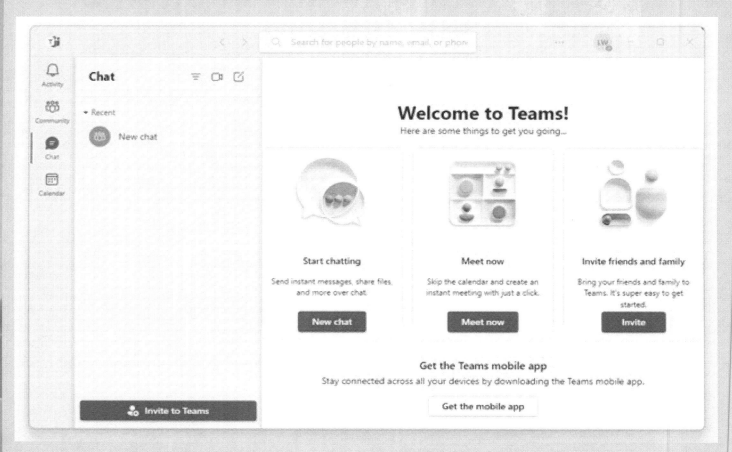

We will then access the main page of Teams, which is divided into four main menus:

- Activity
- Community
- Chat
- Calendar

Now, let's learn how to create a new conversation, schedule a meeting, and invite someone on Teams.

How to create a new conversation

On Teams, you can initiate a new chat with an individual or a group, and the process is the same. Start by selecting the "**New Chat**" icon at the top of the chat list.

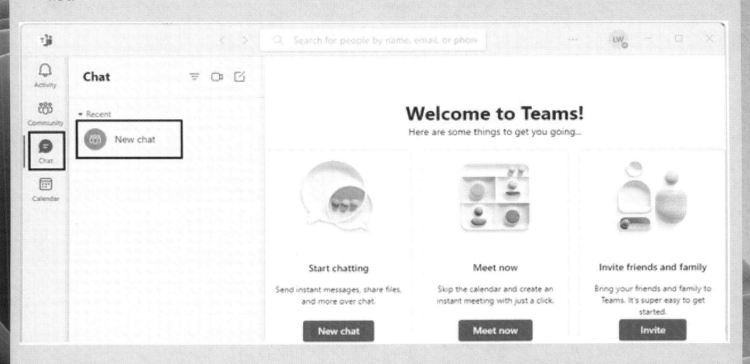

After clicking on the "**New Chat**" icon in Teams and entering the person's name, you can compose your message in the box at the bottom of the chat. To access the formatting options, click on the "**Format**" expand button located below the message input box.

When you are ready, click on the "**Send**" icon or press ENTER to send the message and begin the chat.

 WINDOWS 11 FOR SENIOR

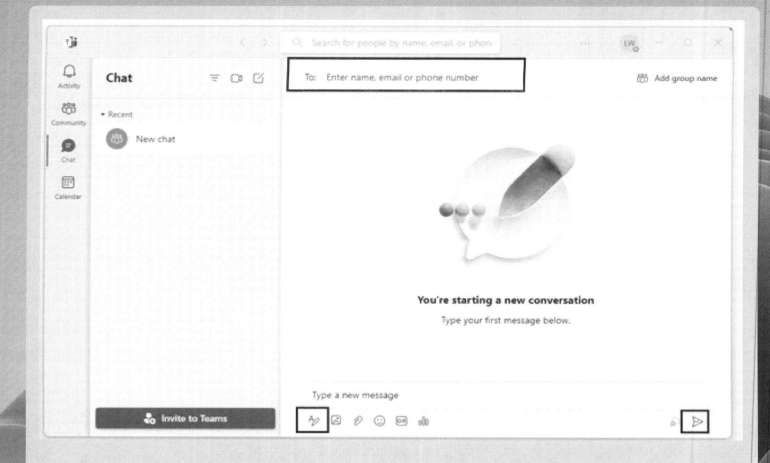

Create a community:

Teams communities provide a centralized platform for connecting with people, engaging in conversations, participating in community video calls, sharing files and photos, managing memberships, and more.

These communities offer a secure environment for sharing, supported by management tools that enable community creators to invite users, establish guidelines for interactions among community members, and enlist assistance in community management.

Creating a community is a simple process. All you need to do is provide a name and a brief description.

 WINDOWS 11 FOR SENIOR

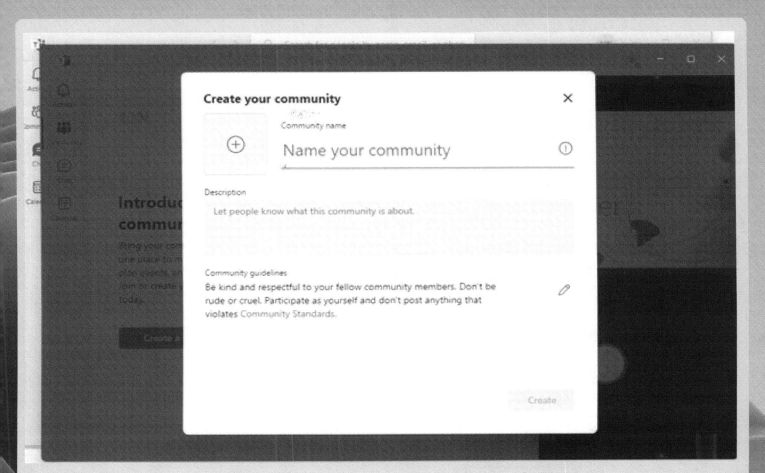

After creating the community, you can invite people to participate by simply clicking on "Invite Members" or by clicking on the person icon in the upper right corner. You can also generate a shareable link that provides access to the community you have created.

For example, in this image, you can see the community I have with my colleagues at the university. Through this community, I can easily share information and news with them.

In turn, community participants can post comments under the posts I publish and create their own posts.

WINDOWS 11 FOR SENIOR

How to create a new meeting

To create a new meeting, go to the chat and click on the camera icon. Give a name to the new meeting you are creating and click on "Start meeting." A link will also be generated that you can share to invite participants, or you can directly invite your contacts to the meeting.

As you can see, creating the meeting is really simple.

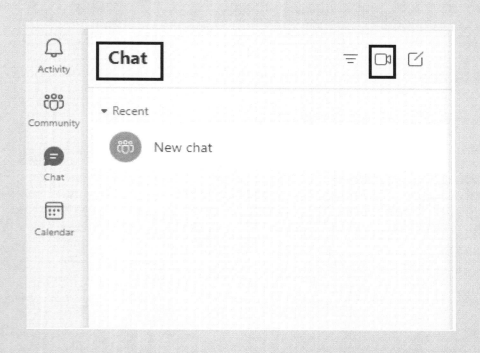

WINDOWS 11 FOR SENIOR

Once you have started the meeting, a new window will open where you can interact with other participants. Let's take a look at all the icons in the meeting window and their functions together.

- The meeting duration is displayed.
- Click to "Chat" to open the meeting chat.
- Click to "People" to view the list of participants and invited attendees.
- Use the "Raise your hand" feature to get the attention of the meeting organizer and request to speak.
- The three buttons provide access to additional meeting settings, such as meeting information, language settings, and background effects (if you want to change your webcam background).
- Click the Camera icon to turn your webcam on or off.
- Click the Mic icon to mute or unmute your microphone.
- Click Share to share your screen.
- Click Leave to exit the meeting, ending it for all participants.

How to use Calendar App in Teams
The "Calendar" section provides a view of your appointments and scheduled meetings. From there, you can also schedule a new meeting by clicking on "New meeting."

A new window will open where you can enter the details of the meeting, such as:

- The name of the meeting
- The contacts of the people to be invited to the meeting
- The date and time of the meeting
- The location of the meeting
- Details and notes of the meeting

 WINDOWS 11 FOR SENIOR

Click on the "**Save**" button to finalize the meeting schedule.

New meeting   Details

Time zone: (UTC+01:00) Amsterdam, Berlin, Bern, Rome, Stockholm, Vienna ∨

ⓘ With your current Teams plan, you get up to 60 minutes per meeting with up to 100 participants. Learn more

✎ Add title

👤 Enter name, email or phone number

🕐 6/4/2023   9:30 PM ∨   →   6/4/2023   10:00 PM ∨   30m ●   All day

🔁 Does not repeat ∨

📍 Add location

≡ **B** *I* U̲ S̶ ∀ A̲ AA Paragraph ∨   ⊟ ⊟ ≡ ⅛ 99 ⇔ ⊟ ⊞ ↺ ↻

Type details for this new meeting

Teams Settings

To customize your Microsoft Teams, access the general settings by clicking on "**Activity**" and "**Settings**." Here, you can set the language, manage app notifications, choose the appearance of Teams, manage your contacts, and even consider upgrading Teams if available.

 WINDOWS 11 FOR SENIOR

10.2 Microsoft To-Do, the Smart Daily Planning

Microsoft To-Do is a task management and to-do list application developed by Microsoft. It is designed to help users organize and keep track of their daily activities, tasks, reminders, and to-do lists.

The app allows users to create custom lists, set deadlines, add notes, and collaborate with others. Windows 11 includes Microsoft To-Do, formerly known as Wunderlist, a free program for managing to-do lists. You can use Microsoft To-Do on your computer, mobile device (with dedicated iOS and Android applications), or online.

To-Do is useful for managing and coordinating your personal and professional responsibilities. It allows you to track events, collections, tasks, and reminders. It's important not to confuse Microsoft To-Do with Microsoft Planner, a project management application included in Windows 11. Microsoft To-Do is cross-platform, allowing you to access it on your desktop PC, iOS or Android device, or through the web for managing your to-do tasks.

To start Microsoft To-Do, type "To Do" in the search bar on the taskbar or type "To Do" after clicking the Start button.

If you are not logged in yet, please log in with your Microsoft account. Once the app launches, you will find the navigation panel on the left side where you can create daily tasks, assign tasks, and more. On the right side, you will find the focus panel. Now let's see how to create, manage, and assign tasks.

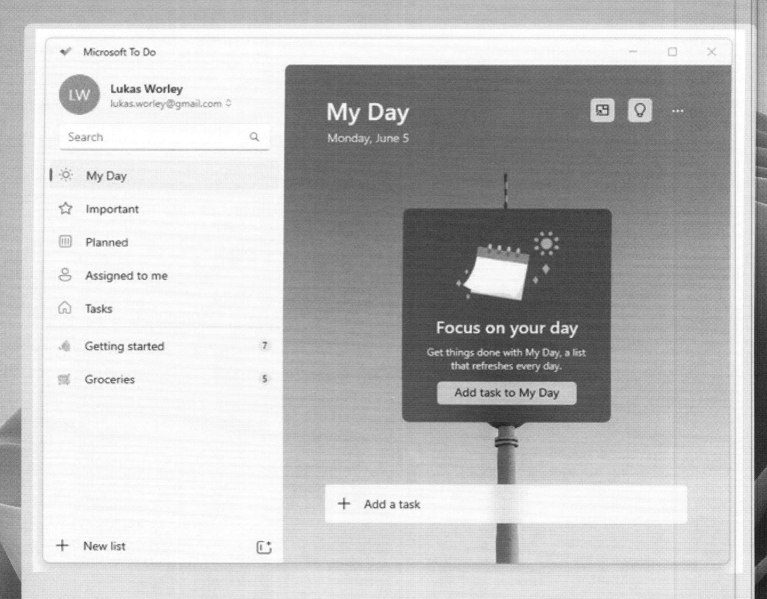

Creating a task

Creating a task is really simple. In the "My Day" section, click on "Add Task," give the task a name, and press Enter on the keyboard to save it. The task you just created will be added to the list of tasks in the My Day section. By clicking on the task, you can perform additional actions. For example, let's say you want to create a task for your networking principles class at the university. You can create the task "Networking Fundamentals Lesson" and once created, you can edit it and add more information. To delete a task, simply click on the trash can icon located in the lower right corner.

 WINDOWS 11 FOR SENIOR

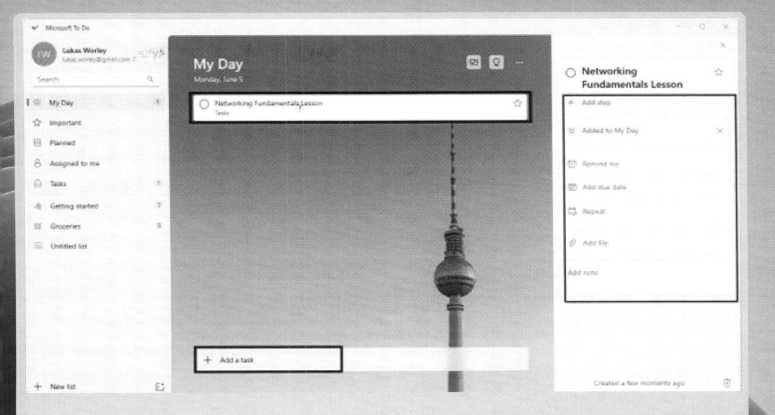

Subtasks

Subtasks are used to divide tasks into smaller steps when there are multiple actions to be performed. In the example we mentioned earlier, you can create three subtasks for your university lecture by adding the three chapters that will be covered in the lecture.

To create subtasks, simply click on the "**Add Steps**" button and give each subtask a name. Press Enter on the keyboard to add the subtask.

Then, you have the option to mark the subtask as completed, delete it, or promote the subtask to a task if it becomes too complex to be considered just a subtask. You will also have the option to enter the date on which the task is due and set a reminder. Additionally, if the task is recurring, you can set it to repeat on a daily, weekly, monthly, or other specified basis.

WINDOWS 11 FOR SENIOR

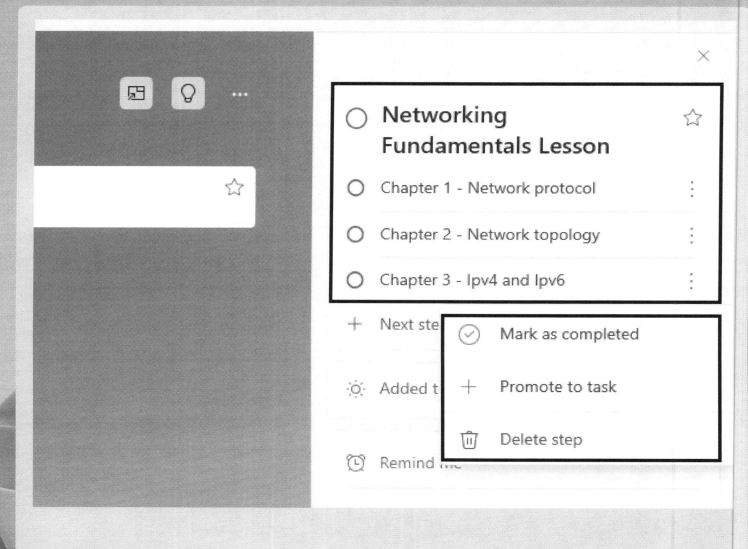

Add File

You can also attach a file to your task, which can be an image, document, text file, etc. To do this, simply click on "Add file," which will open the "File Explorer" for you. From there, you can search for the file you want to add.

Add notes

To add a note, click on "Add note" and enter a small description or note that you want to include with the task.

 WINDOWS 11 FOR SENIOR

Lists and groups

Lists are used to group your tasks, ensuring that they are organized and orderly. To create a list, simply click on the "**New List**" button located in the lower left corner. By default, a list called "Untitled list" will be created, but you can rename it as you like. Once the list is created, you can create new tasks directly within the list (following the steps we discussed earlier) or move existing tasks to the list. To move a task, simply right-click on the task you want to move, then click on "**Move task to**," and select the newly created list.

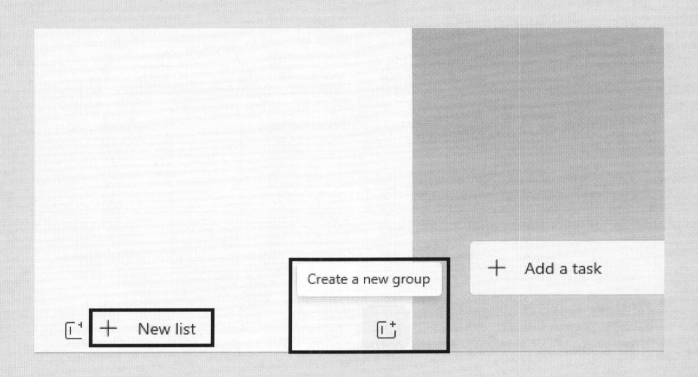

Groups, on the other hand, are used to organize your lists and make your Microsoft To-Do app neat and organized. To create a group, simply click on the "**Create a new group**" button, as shown in the figure.

WINDOWS 11 FOR SENIOR

10.3 How to Take a Screenshot

To capture a screenshot on Windows, you can use two methods:
The first method is to use Windows 11's native capture tool called the **Snipping Tool**.

To start the Snipping Tool:

- Open the Start menu
- Type "snipping tool" into the search box
- Launch the program

Once the Snipping Tool is launched, you can choose whether to take a screenshot of a specific portion of your desktop or record a video of that portion. Simply click on the camera or video camera icon to select your preferred option.

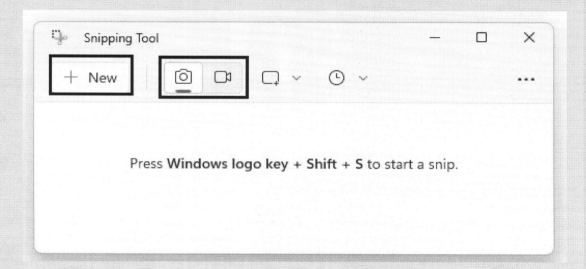

To select the desired portion for capturing, simply click on "New" and then choose the relevant area. It's a straightforward and easy process.
The second method, on the other hand, is much faster but will only allow you to capture a screenshot of your entire desktop using keyboard shortcuts. First, press and hold the PrtSc key. This will capture the entire content on your Windows 11 screen and save it.

 WINDOWS 11 FOR SENIOR

By simply pressing PrtSc, the screenshot will be copied to the clipboard. To create an actual screenshot, you need to paste the picture into an image editor and save the result. Using a timer system requirement for Windows 11 is necessary for capturing any app.

10.4 How to Install Additional Fonts

Although Windows provides us with an enormous amount of fonts, there may be situations where we need a specific font for our documents or small graphic works. Today, I'm going to introduce you to the best website where we can find thousands of amazing and beautiful fonts that can be easily added to our operating system. I'm referring to the dafont site:

www.dafont.com

Log in to the site and search for the font that you like the most. The great thing is that you can already preview the font before downloading it, and to obtain it, simply click on "download." After downloading, you will have a compressed folder (usually a .zip file) that contains the different font styles.

Extract the folder, open the various font files, and simply click on "install."

Once the quick installation process is complete, the font you selected will be available in the font list of all the programs installed on your computer.

 WINDOWS 11 FOR SENIOR

10.5 WhatsApp Desktop

The free messaging program WhatsApp is an excellent way to stay in touch with coworkers, friends, and family, revolutionizing global communication by enabling conversations and sharing digital and visual content. The popular mobile messaging app WhatsApp is also accessible on Windows PCs through the Microsoft Store. In this section, I will explain how to install WhatsApp from the Microsoft Store on Windows 11. The Windows 11 PC supports multiple versions of this app, including the latest WhatsApp beta, which offers additional features compared to the classic app. WhatsApp is available as a free service across all its versions.

Open the Microsoft Store and search for WhatsApp. Click on the WhatsApp icon and then press "Get" to initiate the installation process. Once the installation is complete, WhatsApp will be added to your list of apps. Simply click on it to launch the application.

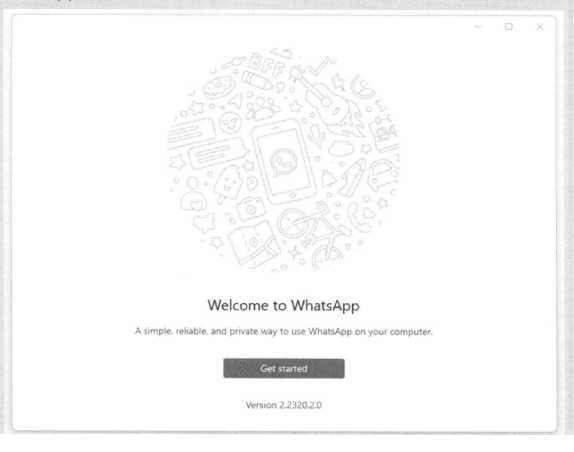

Welcome to WhatsApp

A simple, reliable, and private way to use WhatsApp on your computer.

Get started

Version 2.2320.2.0

 WINDOWS 11 FOR SENIOR

Click "**Get Started**" to begin setting up WhatsApp on your computer. A QR code will be generated, which you'll need to use to link your PC and smartphone. Follow these steps:

1. Open WhatsApp on your smartphone.
2. Tap on the three dots in the top-right corner and go to "Linked Devices." Here, you can check if any devices are already connected to your WhatsApp. If you see any unfamiliar devices, immediately unlink them.
3. Tap on "Link a Device" and scan the QR code displayed on the WhatsApp desktop app.

The linking process will be instant, and after a few seconds, you will see all your conversations appear on the desktop.

10.6 Opening a Second Desktop

Just like in Windows 10, Windows 11 also allows you to have multiple desktops for better organization. This feature is extremely useful as it allows you to keep the same icons on the desktop while having different sets of open windows, folders, or programs on each desktop. This way, you can have separate and organized working environments.

I personally find this feature very convenient. I use one desktop for my work tools and another for leisure programs, and so on.
To view the list of available desktops, simply click on the toolbar icon.

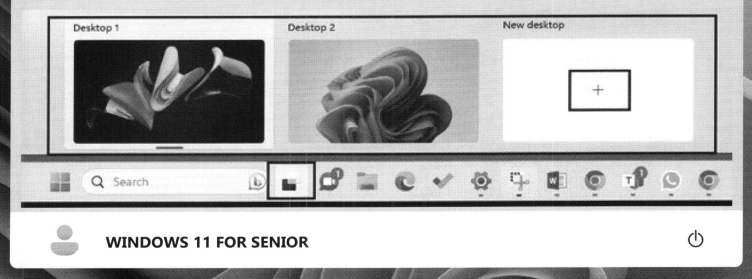

WINDOWS 11 FOR SENIOR

By default, Windows creates two desktop environments right away. If you need a new desktop, simply right-click on the "+" icon in the "New Desktop" section.

10.7 Using and Organizing Calendar App

The built-in Calendar app in Windows 11 enables you to set personal and work-related reminders, meetings, and other events. You can also sync your calendars from other services such as iCloud, Google Calendar, Outlook, and more, with Windows Calendars, allowing you to view all your appointments in one place. The Calendar app can be accessed even without an active internet connection, providing convenience for users who prefer offline access to their calendar or schedule. However, to sync your calendar across multiple devices, you may need to sign in with your Microsoft account.

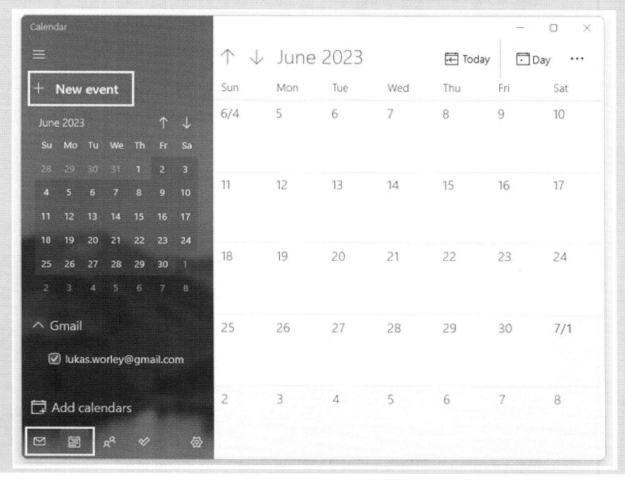

Launch the Calendar App from your start menu (you may notice that you can also switch to the Mail app from within the same app).
Here, you will see all the accounts that you have previously linked to the Mail App, allowing you to manage multiple people's calendars within the same app. In this case, my calendar and events will be highlighted with a color assigned to me.

To create a new event, simply click on the "New event" button. A new tab will open where you can enter the details of the event:
- Event name
- Time and date of the event
- Description of the event
- You will have the option to send the event invitation to other people by entering their email addresses
- You will also be able to view the list of people invited to the event.

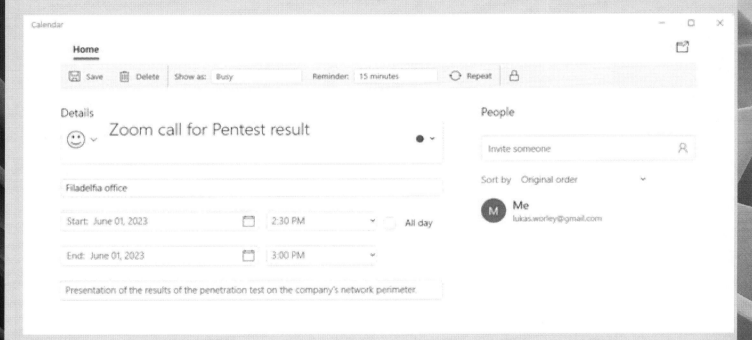

This is one of the most convenient apps that I use every day, as it allows me to stay organized and not miss any appointments or commitments. It helps me keep track of all my events effectively.

 WINDOWS 11 FOR SENIOR

10.8 Write Document With WordPad

WordPad is a word processing program included in the Microsoft Windows operating system. It is a basic application that allows you to create, edit, and format text documents. WordPad offers essential editing features, such as typing and formatting text, changing font type and size, adding images, and creating bulleted or numbered lists.

Unlike Microsoft Word, which is part of the Microsoft Office productivity suite and offers advanced formatting, editing, and document management features, WordPad is a much simpler word processing program. It is generally used for basic tasks such as writing letters, creating lists, or formatting simple documents. WordPad is preinstalled in almost all versions of Windows and can be accessed through the Start menu or by searching the system for it. Despite its limited functionality, WordPad can still be useful for those seeking a quick and easy text editing solution without having to install more complex software such as Microsoft Word or other advanced text editors.

Search for the program in the search bar on your taskbar and open WordPad.

By default, a new blank document is created in which you can immediately start writing your text. In the upper left corner, you will find the File menu.

Clicking on it opens a new window where you can:

- Create a new document
- Open an existing document
- Save the current document
- Print the document
- Send the document via email
- Exit the program

WINDOWS 11 FOR SENIOR

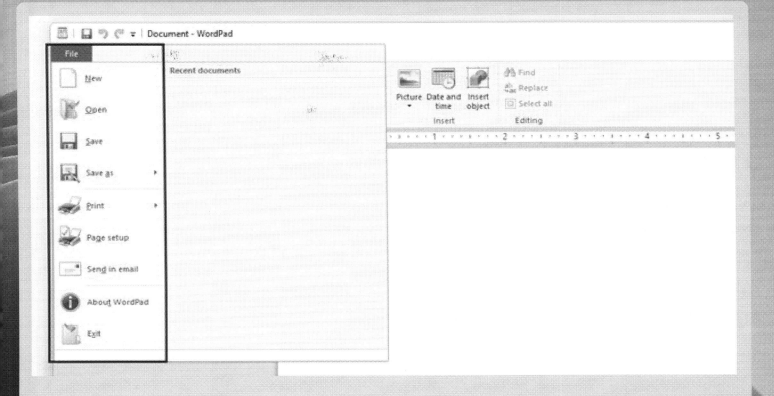

In the Home menu, you have the ability to choose the font to use in your document, the font size and style, and to add images or objects. You can also insert bulleted or numbered lists.

In the View menu, on the other hand, you can zoom in or out on the document and adjust settings such as the measurement system to be used. Additionally, you can choose whether to display the status bar and ruler.

When you type text into a WordPad document, the flashing insertion cursor indicates the precise location of the content. As you reach the end of a line, the text will automatically wrap to the next line below. Unlike a typewriter, you don't need to use the "Enter" key to start a new line within a paragraph. Instead, the "Enter" key in WordPad starts a new paragraph. In WordPad, holding down the "Shift" key and pressing an alphabet key will produce uppercase letters.

To create symbols, you can use a shortcut by holding down the Shift key and pressing the corresponding number button for the symbol you want to make. If you use the "Backspace" key, the letters to the left of the insertion cursor will be erased. Press the Delete (or Del) key to remove characters to the right of the insertion cursor. Alternatively, you can select text for deletion by clicking and dragging over it in WordPad. To remove any selected text or content, simply press the Delete (or Del) key.

WordPad is extremely user-friendly and is likely the ideal solution if you don't have high requirements. However, in the next subchapter, we will explore more advanced free alternatives that you can use if you need professional tools without the need to purchase a license for Microsoft Word.

10.9 Free Alternative to Writing Documents

There is no doubt that Microsoft Word is the most popular word processor, allowing for easy document creation. As a result, the options for alternatives to Microsoft Word may seem limited. However, this widely used word processor has its flaws, such as limited operating system support and the absence of a free version. Many also find it cumbersome and not well-suited for modern applications.

While some people swear by Microsoft Word, others prefer different applications.

If you're seeking a text editor that works across multiple systems and don't want to spend extra money on Microsoft Word's additional features, look no further. Here are some free alternatives to Microsoft Word:

Docs by Google:

Google Docs is a powerful word processor and one of the most well-known alternatives to Microsoft Word. It offers similar features and allows users to create and share files in various formats. Google Docs can be enhanced with different extensions. Despite being hosted online, you can access and edit documents even without an internet connection. It's a great platform for collaborative work, supporting simultaneous teamwork. It's compatible with multiple file types, including PDF, and integrates with Google's G Suite.

LibreOffice:

LibreOffice Writer is an outstanding alternative to Microsoft Word and has been dubbed the "universal word processor" for all types of textual work. It works well with Unix, Mac OS X, and Microsoft Windows. If you're looking for a powerful alternative to Microsoft Word, look no further than LibreOffice Writer. It offers two versions of the text editor, both capable of creating documents using predefined templates and intuitive wizards. It supports importing and exporting various file types and even allows you to convert documents to PDF without needing additional software. LibreOffice is an excellent free alternative to Microsoft Word.

QUIZ
CHAPTER 10

1 - WhatsApp is also available for Windows PCs through the
A)   Microsoft Store
B)   Play store
C)   Prime Video

2 - When the current line reaches its conclusion, the text will automatically
A)   Go down
B)   Back to the beginning
C)   End

3 - In WordPad, tapping the alphabet keys while holding down the "Shift" key produces
A)   Lowercase letters
B)   Uppercase letters
C)   Vowels

4 - What is the easiest way to take a screenshot?
A)   Use the key combination Ctrl + S
B)   Using the native application Snipping Tool
C)   Pressing the F5 key

 WINDOWS 11 FOR SENIOR

5 - From where can you open the Calendar App?

A)   Start menu
B)   Switch from the Mail App
C)   Settings App

Answers

1.   A
2.   B
3.   B
4.   B
5.   A and B

 WINDOWS 11 FOR SENIOR

CHAPTER 11
WINDOWS SECURITY

Virus protection, gadget health, networking, firewalls, online security, app management, and family safety are just some functions that can be managed from the Windows Security center options. Click "All Programs" in the upper right corner of the Start screen. Select "Windows Security" from the drop-down menu. Some of your choices are listed along the left side of the 'home' page and elsewhere:

- **Anti-Malware & Other Threat Defense**. In this location, you may do a thorough system scan that will examine both your computer's files and the system's files and applications for any potential dangers. You may initiate a "secure mode" restart to search for threats offline. If malware persists after a full or fast scan, this scan will eliminate it. Most risks are automatically isolated once they are recognized.

- **Security for Your Account.** Account security settings, device syncing options, Windows Hello sign-in configurations, dynamic lock activation/deactivation.

- **Network Security and Firewalls**. Fix Wi-Fi and internet connection problems, as well as configure the firewall, in this section. The firewall's settings are also accessible.

- **Modify Apps and Web Browsers.** Protect yourself against harmful websites, apps, and downloads by adjusting the settings for your browser and applications like the SmartScreen filter.

 WINDOWS 11 FOR SENIOR

- **Safety of Electronics**. Modify the security settings to enable or deactivate protections against attacks that compromise a process's core isolation and memory integrity.

- **Health and Efficiency of the Device**. The results of any problems with drivers, updates, power, or storage space will be shown here. If Windows 11 isn't performing as expected, you may reinstall it while all your data remains intact using the refresh option.

- **Options for Families**. Here you'll find information on how to use the parental controls on your web browser and keep tabs on what your children are doing online.

- **Preserving Past**. Here you may see what has been done to address possible dangers and what further could be done.

11.1 What Is a Firewall?

To protect your computer, Windows 11 has a firewall called Windows Firewall. Its main function is to prevent malicious connections from being established to your computer and to stop potentially dangerous apps from exchanging data. You may access the firewall settings by clicking the Windows Security shortcut on the start menu. Firewall and Network Protection.

11.2 What Is an Antivirus?

We have seen in Chapter 5.5 how to install one of the best free antivirus programs available online. But now I want to explain to you how a traditional antivirus works and how we can increase our level of security. Everything you will find in this chapter is the result of many years of experience as a cybersecurity expert, and the same advice and tools you will find here are the ones I use for my clients. These are consultations that companies pay hundreds of dollars for, but for you, they will be completely free. Throughout the entire book, you will find tips that will exponentially enhance your security, so make good use of them.

Before I tell you what an antivirus is and how it works, I need to explain what a file's **HASH** is and what is meant by hashing (or hashing algorithm).

Hashing is a function that ensures the integrity and authenticity of data, meaning that it has not been modified or manipulated in any way. Hashing is a mathematical process that takes a file of any type as input and transforms it into a fixed-length string called the file's hash. This process is designed in such a way that even a minor modification of the original file will produce a completely different hash value.

Let's say we have a text file called "**test.txt**" that contains the following text:

"Lorem Ipsum is simply dummy text of the printing and typesetting industry."

If we apply a hash function to the file "test.txt," we will get the following string:

"**6e436ed102721h9b0272eer1f6419f1056c1358c**"

If we modify the file by removing the **dot** at the end, we will get the following hash:

"**d955258326d8d02d6cy805556d8306d19qf32**"

As you can see, a simple modification has resulted in a completely different hash, allowing us to immediately understand that someone has tampered with our file. Furthermore, hashing is a non-invertible process, which means that if I have the hash of a file, I cannot obtain the file that produced it. All these characteristics ensure the integrity and authenticity of the data.

But why this explanation? Because the antivirus is linked to the hash.
The functioning of traditional antivirus programs is based on checking the hashes of files that we execute on our computer every day. Each antivirus vendor (McAfee, AVG, Kaspersky, Panda, etc.) possesses huge databases where all the hashes of malicious files that have been reported are stored.

 WINDOWS 11 FOR SENIOR

These are called "**antivirus signatures**." One of the best practices is to always keep the antivirus signatures up to date because numerous new viruses are reported every day. By constantly updating them, our computer is always protected.

When we execute a file, our antivirus calculates its hash, which is then compared with all the file hashes contained in the databases (the antivirus signatures). If no match is found, it means that the file is not malicious, and the antivirus allows its execution. If a match is found within the signatures, the antivirus blocks the file because it is malicious.

But what happens if a malicious file has not yet been included in the antivirus signatures? The answer is just what you are thinking: your computer will get infected by the virus. However, thanks to this book and what I will tell you now, you can increase your protection level up to 99% with the help of anti-malware.

11.3 What Is an Antimalware?

An antimalware is software that does not rely on checking antivirus signatures (which is a static method) to protect your PC, but instead monitors the behavior of a file when it is executed. Due to this approach, it can detect and intercept any fraudulent behavior exhibited by the executed file, such as data encryption processes or unauthorized communication with so-called command and control servers to download other malicious software. By doing so, it effectively blocks such activities. It's important to note that antimalware is not a substitute for antivirus software, but rather should be used in conjunction with it. This combination will provide you with maximum protection. Now, let me tell you exactly which antimalware software you should use. Scan the QR code below to download Malwarebytes.

Without a doubt, Malwarebytes is the best antimalware software available, and it works exceptionally well even in its free version. By using the AVG + Malwarebytes combination, you can browse the web and download files with greater peace of mind.

11.4 What Is a Sandbox?

Suppose you have downloaded a file, but you are not 100% sure if it is safe and don't want to take the risk of running it on your computer, even with up-to-date antivirus and antimalware protection. There is a method to scan the file in the cloud and quickly determine if it is potentially dangerous. I'm referring to VirusTotal, a highly popular and free website that allows you to upload any file or URL for analysis.

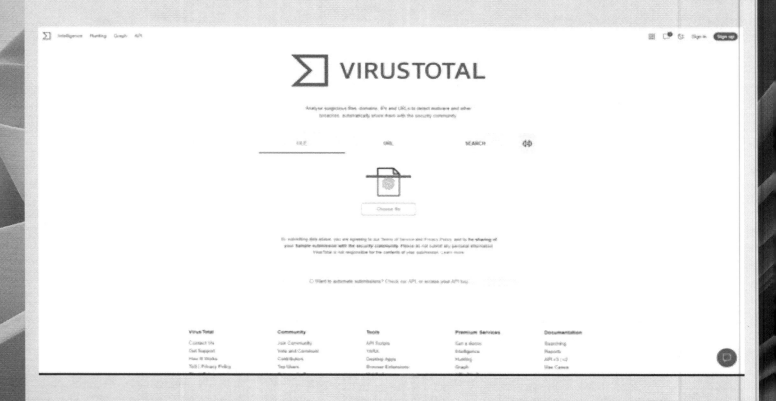

 WINDOWS 11 FOR SENIOR

VirusTotal operates through three main areas:

1. File: You can upload a file to be analyzed.
2. URL: You simply paste a URL, and it will inform you if there are any security threats associated with it.
3. Search: This is a more general search, where you can enter file hashes, IP addresses, and more.

This tool is not widely known among novice or even average users, but I assure you that it is an incredibly useful resource. In large companies, it often plays a crucial role in preventing computer infections, saving them hundreds of thousands of dollars each year.

11.5 Keep Windows Safe by Installing Security Updates

After years of consulting at major U.S. and European companies, I can confidently state that one of the primary reasons why hacker attacks succeed in corporate and home environments is due to people neglecting to keep their antivirus signatures up to date and failing to install routine updates released by Microsoft. This leads to significant security vulnerabilities that jeopardize personal data and can disrupt the functionality of your computer. It is crucial to regularly update your computer's security definitions. Let's now explore how to accomplish this.

Windows Update:

First, let's learn how to check for updates released by Windows and install them. Open the Settings App and navigate to Windows Update.

Windows Update

 You're up to date
Last checked: Today, 12:34 PM

Check for updates

ⓘ 2023-05 Cumulative Update Preview for Windows 11 Version 22H2 for x64-based Systems (KB5026446) is available.   Download & install   ✕

 WINDOWS 11 FOR SENIOR ⏻

In this section, you will find a list of available Windows updates that can be downloaded and installed. If you don't see any updates or wish to check for new ones, simply click on the "Check for updates" button.

The updates you should always prioritize are known as "security updates." These updates protect your system by addressing known vulnerabilities and preventing malicious actors from exploiting them.

Antivirus Signatures

We have already discussed how antivirus software functions and the importance of keeping antivirus definitions up to date. Now, let's delve into the practical steps of updating antivirus signatures. Assuming you have followed my recommendation, you should already have AVG installed, which is considered one of the top free antivirus programs.

Let's now proceed with configuring the automatic updates of antivirus signatures. Although they should already be set as the default option, it's always better to double-check. To do so, click on the "Settings" icon (the small gear-shaped icon located on the right side), then navigate to "**General**" and select "**Update**."
In this section, you can verify that your antivirus is being properly updated and ensure that the antivirus definitions are automatically downloaded and installed.

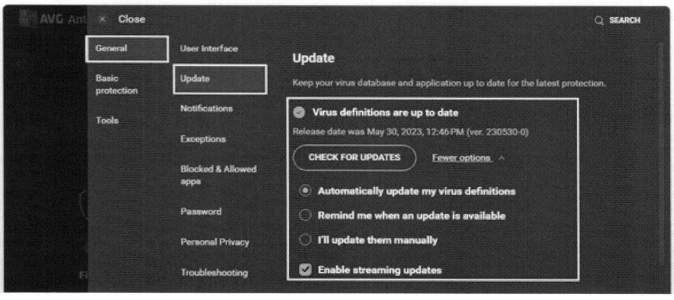

 WINDOWS 11 FOR SENIOR

11.6 Customize Privacy Settings

This subchapter will cover a highly relevant topic that has gained attention recently: privacy. In order for Windows to function optimally and for all installed apps to work effectively, Windows needs to obtain permissions to ensure hardware and software can interact seamlessly, allowing software to utilize hardware automatically.

A classic example is granting permission for our computer to share its location. This is particularly useful when utilizing Windows' "find my device" feature, which helps locate a lost or stolen PC by tracing its GPS coordinates.

Another example involves granting permissions for our webcam to be automatically used by software like Zoom, Teams, or Google Meet.

All privacy settings can be adjusted by navigating to the following path:

Settings App > Privacy & Security.

Privacy & security

Find my device
Track your device if you think you've lost it

For developers
These settings are intended for development use only

Windows permissions

General
Advertising ID, local content, app launches, settings suggestions, productivity tools

Speech
Online speech recognition for dictation and other voice-based interactions

Inking & typing personalization
Custom dictionary, words in your dictionary

Diagnostics & feedback
Diagnostic data, inking and typing data, tailored experiences, feedback frequency

Activity history
Options for getting more from your activity history across devices and accounts

Search permissions

 WINDOWS 11 FOR SENIOR

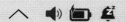

Here, we can review the permissions we have knowingly or unknowingly granted to various apps. We can grant new permissions or revoke existing ones by simply toggling the switches on and off, as demonstrated in the figure for camera sharing permissions.

Privacy & security › **Camera**

The settings on this page do not prevent you from signing in with your camera using facial recognition (Windows Hello). Some desktop apps might not appear on this page or be affected by these settings. **Learn more about camera**

📷	**Camera access** Anyone using this device can choose if their apps have camera access when this is on	On ⬤
☰	**Let apps access your camera** Choose which apps can access your camera	On ⬤ ∧
	Camera	On ⬤
	Desktop App Web Viewer	Off ○
	Feedback Hub	On ⬤
	Microsoft Store	On ⬤
	Windows Feature Experience Pack	On ⬤
	Xbox	On ⬤
	Xbox Game Bar	On ⬤
	Let desktop apps access your camera Desktop apps that have previously accessed your camera are listed here	On ⬤

11.7 How to Lock Your Computer
You may have never thought about it, but one of the most frequently used methods of stealing personal data is precisely by exploiting unlocked computers.

 WINDOWS 11 FOR SENIOR

It's always a good idea to lock your PC when you're not using it to prevent unauthorized access to your files, applications, and sensitive information. By locking your computer, you can ensure that nobody can access your system without entering your password or biometric authentication if enabled. Additionally, if you work in a shared space or office, locking your computer can prevent others from accessing your files or data when you're away from your desk.

To lock your Windows 11 computer, you can use any of the following methods:

1. Press the Windows key + L
2. Click on the Start menu and click on your user icon, then select "Lock"
3. Press Ctrl + Alt + Del and select "Lock"

11.8 Windows Security Settings

Antivirus software, or Microsoft Defender Antivirus, is already included in Windows as part of Windows Security. (Windows Security is known as Windows Defender Security Manager in early builds of Windows 10). Microsoft Defender Antivirus can disable itself immediately if you have another antivirus program running. Once the conflicting program is deleted, Microsoft Defender Antivirus will restart itself.

Microsoft Defender is a security solution developed by Microsoft that provides antivirus and anti-malware protection for Windows-based computers and devices. Microsoft Defender Antivirus is a built-in feature of Windows (starting with the version of Windows 10) that provides real-time protection against viruses, malware, spyware, and other types of threats. It uses a combination of signature-based and behavioral-based detection to identify and block malicious files and processes. It also includes features such as firewall and network protection, controlled folder access, and exploit protection.

Within this book, I have already shown you other (free) antivirus and anti-malware solutions because in my daily experience with Windows, Microsoft Defender has some flaws and has often performed less well than other Antivirus solutions.

NB: Just for your technical knowledge, to evaluate and analyze the various vendors in the market, of a given industry or service, one uses the "Gartner Magic Quadrant," which is a chart that illustrates the positioning of one product relative to another.

Windows Security is the hub from which you can control all of your computer's and data's security features, Detect and remove viruses and other malware with real-time protection that constantly monitors for new threats and installs updates. Safeguard your account by adjusting your sign-in preferences and activating security features like Windows Hello and dynamic lock. Manage your firewall's settings and keep tabs on your networks and online activity for optimal security. Modify Microsoft Defender SmartScreen's settings to safeguard your device against malicious software, web content, and downloadable files.

Your devices will be protected against exploits, and you may adjust the level of security as needed. Protecting your device from malicious software requires that you make use of its built-in security features. Keep your device clutter-free and run the most recent version of Windows for optimal performance and health. Options for the whole family to monitor the usage of electronic devices and the time spent online by children.

QUIZ
CHAPTER 11

1 - Microsoft has not made it simple to turn it off permanently
A)   Firewall
B)   Defender
C)   Antivirus

2 - What are the Antivirus Signatures
A)   They are antivirus plug-ins
B)   These are text strings that uniquely represent a file that will then be matched against the antivirus signature database
C)   They are advanced antivirus engines that rely on the behavior of the file.

3 - To always remain safe from possible external manacles, it is important to
A)   Never connect to the internet via W-Fi
B)   Make constant security updates of Windows
C)   Turn up the Firewall security

4 - Where are the privacy and security settings?
A)   Settings App > Privacy & Security
B)   Control Panel > Privacy & Security
C)   Settings App > Security & Privacy

 WINDOWS 11 FOR SENIOR

5 - What does an antivirus rely on to tell if a file is malicious?

A)   The file extension

B)   The file size

C)   The file hash

Answers

1.   B
2.   B
3.   B
4.   A
5.   A

 WINDOWS 11 FOR SENIOR

CHAPTER 12
NETWORKING

Networking refers to the practice of connecting multiple devices, such as computers, phones, and tablets, so that they can communicate and exchange information.

For example, when you are connected to a Wi-Fi network, your device connects to a router, which in turn is connected to other devices, such as computers or printers that share the same network. This connection between devices allows you to exchange data, such as files or emails, and access shared resources, such as a printer or file server.

Network networking can be used in both home and business environments, where sharing resources and information is critical for efficiency and productivity. Creating a computer network enables more efficient use of resources and simplifies data and information management.

In Windows 11 you may change your Wi-Fi or Ethernet connection parameters under the menu labeled "**Network & internet**".

In this part of the book we will look together at what the most important parts of the networking section of Windows are and some tricks for optimizing the performance and security of our home network.

 WINDOWS 11 FOR SENIOR

Network & internet

Wi-Fi
Connected, secured

Properties
Public network
5 GHz

Data usage
6.21 GB, last 30 days

Wi-Fi — Connect, manage known networks, metered network	On	>
Ethernet — Authentication, IP and DNS settings, metered network		>
VPN — Add, connect, manage		>
Mobile hotspot — Share your internet connection	Off	>
Airplane mode — Stop wireless communication	Off	>
Proxy — Proxy server for Wi-Fi and Ethernet connections		>
Dial-up — Set up a dial-up internet connection		>
Advanced network settings — View all network adapters, network reset		>

12.1 Workgroups

Microsoft Windows's built-in workgroup network allows users to communicate with one another in a decentralized manner. Shared resources and access to each other are only possible amongst computers in the same workgroup, which requires that they all be part of the same LAN. To share files, printers, etc., between two machines on the same local network, each must have the same Workgroup name.

When you create a workgroup in Windows, all the computers that are part of it can easily see and access each other's shared resources. When Windows 11 is installed, PCs are placed in a predefined workgroup named "Workgroup." Follow these procedures to move your PC to a new workgroup.

 WINDOWS 11 FOR SENIOR

- To begin, press the "Start" button.
- Go to the Computer Name tab and click the Change button to rename your computer or switch its domain or workgroup.
- Rename your workgroup in the "Member of" section's Workgroup field.
- To apply the changes, restart your computer after clicking the OK button.

12.2 Domains

This specific section can be a little complex for novice users, and this book is not intended to be too difficult. For this reason, I will only explain what they are for for your culture and interest, but we will not go into the details of how they are created and how they work.

In Windows 11, a domain is a group of computers and devices that are joined together to form a network controlled by a central server, known as a domain controller. Domains are typically used in business environments to provide centralized management of user accounts, security policies, and network resources such as files and printers.

When a computer or device joins a domain, it becomes part of the network and can access resources that are shared within the domain. This includes files, folders, and applications that are available to users on the network.
Domains provide several benefits over workgroups, including enhanced security, centralized management of user accounts and permissions, and simplified access to network resources. They are often used in larger organizations with many users and devices to manage, but can also be used in smaller environments depending on the needs of the organization.

12.3 Static and Dynamic IP address

Within a network, such as our home network, each device that we connect to our modem/router is automatically issued an IP address that identifies the device within that network. This is done by the DHCP server, which I will tell you about shortly.

Launch the Settings menu to get a Dynamic address when using Windows 11. You may accomplish this by selecting it from the Menu Bar or pressing the Windows key plus the letter. The second step is to enter the Settings menu and choose "**Network & Internet**" from the left menu. Next, choose "**Ethernet & Wi-Fi**" from the "Network & Internet" submenu in the Control Panel. An IP address that changes automatically with Windows 11. Afterward, go to the "**IP assignment**" settings by clicking the "**Edit**" button. Choose "**Automatic (DHCP)**" from the "Edit IP Settings" menu, and then click "**Save**." IP address change notification in Windows 11.

With Windows 11, you may set a static IP address in the Settings menu.

- Launch Windows 11's Configuration menu.
- Select the Internet and Network tab.
- Select the Wi-Fi menu item.
- Go with the active connection.
- To modify your IP address settings, use the "Edit" tab.
- Choose the "Manual" setting.
- Engage the IPv4 switch.

12.4 DHCP

Dynamic Host Configuration Protocol (DHCP) is a network system that simplifies the process of connecting devices to a network like the Internet. It automatically assigns network settings such as IP address, subnet mask, and default gateway to devices that join the network, instead of requiring users to manually enter these settings.

DHCP makes network connections quicker and more convenient, especially in networks with many devices, such as in business or home settings.

Navigate to the "Network" tab in your system's properties. A network option, such as Wi-Fi, must be chosen.

- To go to the properties menu, you'll need to click it.
- IP address and DNS server information may be found further down the page. In most cases, leaving them at their default setting of automatic (DHCP) is OK, but there are exceptions.
- Your device's IP address allows other computers on the internet to locate it. Domain names are translated to numerical IP addresses by the domain name server.
- Where it says "IP assignment," click "edit." It is where you'll make changes to the IP address.
- Pick "manual," then fill in the network info.
- Edit the field labeled "DNS server assignment" to adjust the domain name system. Choose "manual," then type in the DNS server's IP address. If you're having trouble with your DNS, try Cloudflare. 1.1.1.3 and 1.0.0.3

QUIZ
CHAPTER 12

1 - Microsoft Windows's built-in workgroup network allows users to _____ with one another in a decentralized manner

A)   Communicate

B)   Link

C)   enable

2 - To get a Dynamic address when using Windows 11, launch the

A)   Start menu

B)   Settings menu

C)   Main menu

3 - When prompted to confirm the changes to the computer's name or domain, choose

A)   Yes

B)   OK

C)   Try Again

4 - From where can you change the Wi-Fi or Ethernet connection parameters in Windows 11?

A)   Network & internet

B)   Ethernet

C)   Wi-Fi connection

 WINDOWS 11 FOR SENIOR

5 - If you're having trouble with your DNS, try

A)   Cloudflare. 1.1.1.3 and 1.0.0.3
B)   Cloudflare. 1.1.1.2 and 1.0.0.4
C)   Cloudflare. 1.1.1.1 and 1.0.0.8

Answers

1.   A
2.   B
3.   B
4.   A
5.   A

CHAPTER 13
HOW TO USE WINDOWS FOR FUN

Who's to say that we can't use Windows 11 to entertain ourselves and enjoy some leisure time with good music, movies, or video games?

The Microsoft Store offers tens of thousands of apps available for download, including a wide range of categories such as gaming, productivity, and health. You can find programs for everything from gaming and media consumption to serious work in word processing, design, and illustration. Additionally, there are useful tools like the calculator and various unit conversion apps for length, volume, currency, and more. Exploring the App Store is definitely worth it. In addition to the apps available in the store, Windows also comes with pre-installed programs such as navigation, weather, news, photos, movies, and music.

13.1 Game Mode

When it comes to gaming, Windows 11 offers a Game Mode feature. According to Microsoft, enabling this mode will halt all other background processes and applications, ensuring that you are not interrupted by work applications or other games while playing. As a result, games can be played at a faster pace compared to the default settings. Switching to Game Mode is quite easy.

Simply open the Settings App, navigate to Gaming, and select Game Mode.

 WINDOWS 11 FOR SENIOR

Game Mode
Optimize your PC for play by turning things off in the background
More about Game Mode   On ⬤

Related settings

🖼 Graphics   ›

🔾 Get help

⌨ Give feedback

13.2 Xbox Game Pass

If you own an Xbox and want to play Xbox games on your PC, you can subscribe to Xbox Game Pass and enjoy unlimited gaming. With Xbox Game Pass, you can experience the latest games from Xbox Game Developers and other studios on the day of their release. Similar to Netflix, Microsoft regularly adds and removes games from the service.

For Windows users, Xbox Game Pass is available in two options:

- Game Pass for Xbox One and Windows 10 PCs costs $9.99 per month. This subscription grants you access to a wide selection of fantastic games that can be played exclusively on your PC. It also includes EA Play, which offers access to some of EA's best games, exclusive in-game rewards, and early access to upcoming games.

- The Xbox One Ultimate Game Pass is available for $19.99 per month. With this subscription, you can enjoy Xbox Game Streaming and access games on your Xbox, PC, and other devices. You can even switch between devices and share your progress with others. Additionally, the Ultimate membership includes Xbox Live Gold, which allows for online multiplayer gameplay and provides special discounts.

Choose the Xbox Game Pass option that suits your needs and enjoy a vast library of games across multiple platforms.

 WINDOWS 11 FOR SENIOR   ⏻

13.3 Android Games

Anyone in the United States or anywhere else now has the opportunity to test Google's pre-release preview of Android games on Windows 11 PCs. Earlier this year, the company introduced a beta version of a program that allowed users in certain locations, including Taiwan, Hong Kong, and South Korea, to play Android games on their personal computers. However, starting from November 2, anyone in the US, Canada, Mexico, Brazil, Australia, the Netherlands, Malaysia, or Singapore can try out the games in beta form. Currently, only a select few games such as 1946 Air Force, Blades Idle, Biscuit Run: Kingdom, and Evony: The King's Return are playable on the service. Although there are currently only 85 available games, Google promises to introduce more in the future.

To access Google Play Games, you will need a Windows 11 PC with SSD storage, Intel UHD Graphics 630 or above, a CPU with at least four cores, and 8GB of RAM. Additionally, your computer must be configured to use virtualization software.

13.4 Microsoft Store Account Settings

We have previously discussed what the Microsoft Store is and how it can be our primary choice for downloading and installing the software we require. Now, let's delve into a more comprehensive understanding of how it functions and the most effective ways to utilize it.

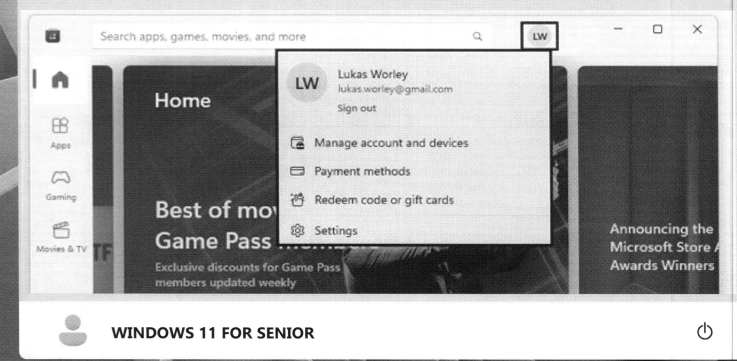

Manage account and device

It allows you to access your Microsoft profile, manage associated devices, and control payment methods in case you want to purchase programs available on the store that are not free. Furthermore, it provides you with complete control over your Microsoft account, enabling you to manage all privacy and security features associated with your account.

Payment methods

Go to the Billing settings page in your Microsoft account settings. If you encounter login problems, fixing your Microsoft account should be your first step. To add a new payment method, click the corresponding button. Select the desired payment method, fill in the required fields, and click the Save button.

Redeeming Codes

To redeem a code or gift card, click on the profile icon at the top of the app and then select the appropriate option. Enter the 25-character code and click on Redeem to complete the process.

13.5 Navigating the Microsoft Store

If you are using Windows 11, you can access the online Microsoft Store by clicking on the store icon located in the system tray. The home screen of the store displays various categories of applications, including featured apps, must-have apps, free games, best free apps, trending applications, and collections. You can find apps, games, and media in their respective dedicated sections within the Microsoft Store.

Apps

To browse through the available free and premium applications, click on the Apps button in the left sidebar. The website is divided into several categories for different purposes, such as sales, top applications, productivity, and collections.

  229

Gaming

If you are looking for downloadable free and paid games, select the Gaming icon on the left and scroll down the page. Here, you will find top-selling games, featured games, free games, premium games, and compilations.

Movies & TV

If you're searching for a movie or TV program to watch, select the TV & Movies tab from the left menu. By scrolling down the page, you can explore what's new, what's highlighted, what's popular, and what's included in collections.

13.6 Have fun with video

One of the main ways to entertain yourself with your device is undoubtedly by watching a good movie or series. In the Microsoft Store, there are two apps that we highly recommend for our entertainment: Amazon Prime Video and Netflix. Amazon Prime Video and Netflix are two popular video streaming services that offer a wide selection of movies, TV series, and other audiovisual content for online viewing. Both services provide users with access to an extensive library of content through a monthly or annual subscription. Amazon Prime Video is part of Amazon's Prime package and includes additional benefits like free shipping and access to music and reading services. Netflix, on the other hand, is an independent streaming service that focuses solely on providing on-demand video content. Both services allow users to enjoy their favorite shows and movies on various devices, including computers, smartphones, tablets, and smart TVs, offering a flexible and convenient entertainment experience.

Amazon Prime Video

Amazon Prime Video is available for free in the Microsoft Store, so all you need to do is search for the app in the store and download it.

To access Amazon Prime Video, you must have an Amazon Prime account, so make sure you have one ready as you will need to enter your login credentials when you launch the app for the first time. After logging in, you will have unlimited access to all Prime content, including TV series, movies, and live sporting events. All you need to do is choose what to watch and enjoy your moments of relaxation.

Netflix

The Netflix app is also available for free in the Microsoft Store, and once again, you must have an active Netflix account.

To enjoy Netflix, you can choose a subscription plan that is divided into various rates. Each plan offers different advantages compared to the cheaper ones, such as the ability to watch content in 4K quality or download the content for offline viewing.

Simply select the subscription plan you prefer and start using Netflix. The library of content is virtually unlimited.

13.7 Have fun with music

Music is the electrical soil in which the spirit lives, thinks, and invents [cit. Ludwig van Beethoven]. This quote is one of my favorites, and music accompanies many moments of our day. Windows 11 offers a variety of apps for listening to our favorite songs, but in my opinion, the best one is undoubtedly Spotify. Let's explore it together and learn more about it.

Spotify

Spotify is a popular music streaming service that allows you to listen to a wide range of songs, albums, and artists from around the world. With Spotify, you can access a vast music library directly from your device, whether you're using a computer, smartphone, or tablet. It provides you with virtually unlimited access to millions of tracks across various genres, enabling you to enjoy your favorite music anytime, anywhere.

The Spotify app is available for free download from the Microsoft Store. Once you have installed it, launch the app and enter your login credentials. You will need to have a Spotify account to access the service. However, if you prefer not to create a dedicated Spotify account, you can also log in using your Google, Apple, or Facebook account. This allows for a convenient login process without the need to create additional credentials specifically for Spotify.

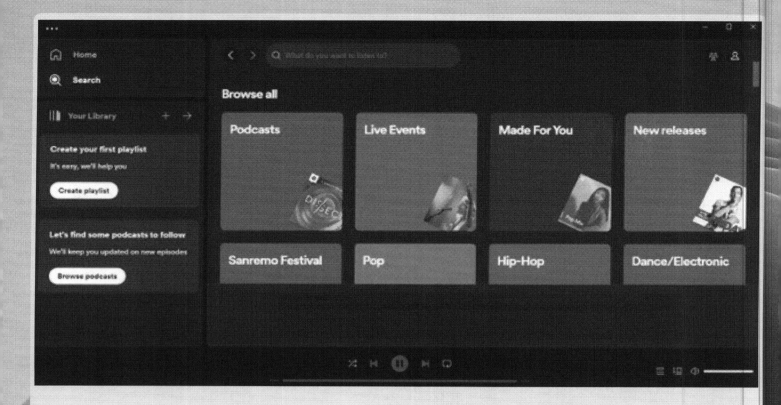

The operation of Spotify is straightforward and user-friendly. By clicking on the "Search" option, you can easily search for any song or artist you wish to listen to. Additionally, you have the option to create your own playlists or explore and listen to playlists that have been curated by other Spotify users. Simply sit back and enjoy your favorite music effortlessly.

13.8 Using the Photo App

The Windows 11 Photo app is an application integrated into the operating system that allows you to view, manage, and edit photos on your device. It offers various features to intuitively organize, share, and enhance your images.

Here's how the Windows 11 Photo app works:

- **Viewing photos**: You can open the Photo app to view the photos stored on your device. The app organizes the photos based on the date they were taken, and you can easily scroll through them.

- **Editing photos**: The Photo app provides basic editing tools to enhance your photos. You can adjust the brightness, contrast, saturation, and apply preset filters to achieve interesting effects.

- **Creating videos**: With the Photo app, you can create videos using your photos. You can select the pictures, add transition effects, background music, and even text to create engaging slideshows.

- **Organizing photos**: The app allows you to create albums to organize your photos based on specific themes or events. This helps you quickly find the desired images without having to search through a large collection.

- **Sharing photos**: Sharing your photos is made easy with the Photo app. You can send images via email, text messages, or directly share them on social media platforms from within the app.

The Windows 11 Photo app aims to provide a user-friendly and intuitive experience for managing your photos. You can explore its features and experiment with different options to customize your images according to your preferences. The Photo app in Windows 11 is the default application used to open photos. To access the app, you can simply type "Photos" in the search bar or click on the "Start" button and then select the Photos app icon.

 **WINDOWS 11 FOR SENIOR**

When you launch the Photos app, it will automatically display all the photos available on your computer. Additionally, it provides easy integration with OneDrive or iCloud, allowing you to access your cloud-stored photos seamlessly. Furthermore, you have the option to create custom folders within the app to organize your photos into specific albums. This allows you to categorize and group your photos based on your preferences (more details on how to do this will be provided later).

13.9 Editing Pictures

Image editing is incredibly easy and fast. First, open the photo you want to edit, and then click on the "**Edit image**" button, as illustrated in the picture.

A new window will open that contains all the tools you need to modify the photo, including:

- **Crop**: This tool allows you to crop the photo.

- **Adjustments**: You can use this tool to adjust the brightness, contrast, and exposure of the image.

- **Filters**: This tool enables you to apply pre-made filters to the photo, giving it the desired effect.

- **Markup**: This tool allows you to draw on the photo and add annotations.

- **Save as copy**: With this option, you can save a copy of the edited photo.

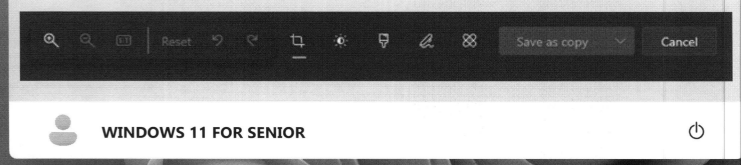

13.10 Create a Photo Album

Creating a photo album is a straightforward task. Simply open the "File Explorer" and navigate to the Pictures folder.

From there, you can create a new folder (as we have previously discussed) and give it the desired name. Then, you can add the photos that belong to this album by placing them inside the folder. With these simple steps, you have successfully created a new photo album.

The album will be automatically synchronized with the Photos app, allowing you to view its contents seamlessly.

13.11 How to Print Your Photo

Open the photo you wish to print and then click on the "**Print**" button. Alternatively, you can use the keyboard shortcut by pressing **Ctrl + P**.

This will open a new window displaying the print settings. Review them carefully, and once you are certain about printing the photo, click on the "**Print**" button to proceed.

13.12 Create a Slideshow

The Slideshow feature on Windows 11 allows you to automatically display a slideshow of images on your device. You can select a series of photos and customize the duration of each image, transition effects between them, and even add background music. During the Slideshow, you have the option to pause, resume, or stop the playback of images. You can also navigate forward or backward through the pictures using the directional arrows on the keyboard. The Slideshow feature provides a convenient way to enjoy a sequence of photos without the need to manually scroll through each image. It is perfect for showcasing your favorite photos during meetings, events, or creating an engaging visual experience on your Windows 11 device.

To start a slideshow, log into the Photos app, select the folder where you want to begin the slideshow, and click on the "**Start Slideshow**" button or press the **F5** key.

 WINDOWS 11 FOR SENIOR

13.13 Microsoft Lens

Office Lens is a convenient tool for capturing text from various flat surfaces, such as whiteboards, menus, signs, and handwritten notes. It eliminates the need for taking manual notes, relying on low-quality photos, or worrying about losing important information. Additionally, it works well for saving non-text images like sketches, drawings, and mathematical formulas. Office Lens automatically removes shadows and corrects skewed perspectives, resulting in clearer and more legible photos. You can scan whiteboards and documents using Word, PowerPoint, OneNote, or OneDrive, and save them as PDFs or email them to others.

Due to the success of Office Lens, Microsoft has rebranded it as "Microsoft Office Lens." The app is now integrated into the Microsoft suite, without any mention of "Office." A new version of the program, called "Microsoft Lens," is currently in development. This new version will retain all the features of the original Office Lens, with plans for additional capabilities in the near future. Microsoft aims to provide a more efficient document scanning solution that simplifies the organization of scanned files.

QUIZ
CHAPTER 13

1 - Which of the following actions cannot be done with La Photo App?
A)   Edit photos
B)   Change photos extension
C)   Creating videos
D)   Sharing photos
E)   Viewing photos

2 - When you're done making selections, hit the
A)   Start button
B)   Save button
C)   detail button

3 - What key combinations can you use to print a photo?
A)   Ctrl + R
B)   Ctrl + P
C)   Win + P

4 - From where do you access the Game Mode?
A)   Settings App
B)   File Explorer
C)   BIOS

5 - Is the Microsoft Store free of charge?

A)   Is always free, but some software inside may be chargeable

B)   Yes

C)   No

Answers

1.   B
2.   B
3.   B
4.   A
5.   A

 WINDOWS 11 FOR SENIOR

CHAPTER 14
WINDOWS 11 TROUBLESHOOTING

Regular computer servicing ensures that your device continues to function properly, protecting your data with anti-virus software, regularly backing up your modern, up-to-date computing system. More technical concerns include defragmenting files, disk cleanups, and startup applications. When your computer crashes, you need a plan to back up and restore your data. There is an automated error-checking and fixing tool integrated into Windows 11. If you're having issues with your computer, check out the Windows 11 troubleshooter website for help.

In addition to fixing your computer problems, MiniTool Software also sells valuable programs like MiniTool Fast Data Recovery and MiniTool Partition Wizard, among others. I will also show you the best free tool to perform a deep cleaning of your PC in order to keep it performing at its best.

14.1 Error Messages, Crash, and Freezing Issue
Users report that doing a RAM test in Windows may resolve the sporadic freezing issue in Windows 11.

To perform this test, here are the simple steps you need to take:

- First, hit Win + R, then enter **mdsched.exe** and hit **OK**.
- Select the first option, "**Restart immediately and check for issues**" (recommended), from the pop-up box.

- Windows 11 will restart and do the check.

RAM is not a problem if you have not found any faults, good news for you!

14.2 Booting in Safe Mode

To access Settings in Windows 11:

- Press the Windows key + I on the keyboard.
- If it doesn't do the trick, go to the Start menu and pick the Settings option.
- Pick Recovery from the list of options under Update & Security.
- Select Restart Now from the menu labeled Advanced Startup.

On the Pick an Options page that appears after the computer has restarted choose Troubleshoot, Advanced Options, Startup Settings, and finally, Restart. After the system has restarted, a menu of choices will be shown. Press the number 4 or the F4 key to boot into Safe Mode. Safe Mode plus Networking may be accessed by pressing F5 or 5.

Many people are terrible at turning off their computers. If problems arose while it was in "sleep" mode, however, we put it to sleep. Regularly powering down a computer running Windows 11 might help it last longer and avoid potential health problems. To open Windows, use the Windows key. To power down, pick the battery symbol from the taskbar.

Checking for New Versions

One potential solution to Windows 11 crashes is to look for updates. Don't wait to upgrade if Microsoft has released a patch to solve the issue. It's also a good idea to check if any updates are available for your PC. If available, check for software and hardware upgrades by locating the OEM update app.

To manually check for the Windows 11 update, follow these steps: Go to Start > Settings > Windows Update and click on the "Check for updates" button. Look for the third Windows 11 upgrade.

 WINDOWS 11 FOR SENIOR

Verify Potentially Incompatible Devices

It's important to note that Windows 11 may also crash due to malfunctioning or incompatible hardware. To rule out this possibility, you can start by checking your PC's peripherals. For example, try removing any docking stations or high-end gaming accessories such as joysticks, microphones, or speakers that could potentially be causing issues.

Ensure that Your Drivers Are Up to Date

A faulty driver may be responsible for Windows 11 freezing and restarting unexpectedly. An unstable system is usually the result of an operating system update, but a problem with a driver may also cause it to occur later. Try installing the most recent version of the device drivers to see if it helps.

Here's how you can accomplish that:

- Access the "Quick Links" menu by pressing Windows + X, and then select "Device Manager."
- Expand the "Disk drives" submenu, and then right-click your disk. Select "Update driver" from the resulting menu.
- From the pop-up menu, select "Search automatically for drivers." Windows 11 will automatically download and install updates, and then prompt you to restart the computer if available.
- If an updated version is not yet available via the Device Manager, you can download the graphics driver from the manufacturer's website. Before downloading a driver, ensure that it is compatible with your graphics card model.

PC overheating

Overheating Windows 11 PCs is a surefire way to make them malfunction. Windows has a built-in safety feature that shuts it down if it becomes too hot, preventing permanent damage to its components. Your computer may overheat if you use it for long periods for gaming, work, streaming, etc. Therefore, on the one hand, you may allow it to cool down before using it again.

 WINDOWS 11 FOR SENIOR

However, if you suspect a problem with heat dissipation, check that the system has enough ventilation, and that the fans are operational. Ensure that it is free of dust by blowing it out with canned air. If you assemble the PC yourself, make sure the heatsinks are secure.

Restore Corrupted System Files by Using DISM and SFC Scan

Windows 11 crashes could be due to corrupted system files. You can repair the OS by using SFC and DISM tools. To check and fix any damaged Windows system files, right-click the Start button and select "Windows Terminal (Admin)."

- Type "Online DISM/Cleanup-Image/Restore Health" in the terminal and press Enter.
- After the DISM scan is complete, use "SFC/scan now."
- The process takes some time (you can treat yourself to a good cup of coffee). After it's finished, restart Windows 11 and check if it still freezes or crashes.
- Use DISM and SFC to restore corrupted system files and reduce software incompatibilities.

Running too many programs simultaneously in the background may cause Windows 11 to malfunction. Other programs, such as OneDrive, Dropbox, or your web browser, could be interfering with the print screen feature. The first step to resolving any software conflicts that may occur is to turn off these background programs. To open Task Manager in Windows 11, use the keyboard shortcut Ctrl + Alt + Delete. To identify the offending process, go to the Processes menu and try to terminate each one. Right-click on the program you want to end and choose "End task." Adjust the software incompatibilities accordingly.

Reboot Your Computer

You may not know this, and it may sound unbelievable, but **80% of the problems you encounter on Windows** can be solved by a simple system restart. During my early years as an IT systems engineer, when I would receive a support call about issues on workstations (which were all Windows XP), the standard response was "Reboot the PC and let me know if it works now." And 100% of the time, the problem was resolved.

 WINDOWS 11 FOR SENIOR

If your Windows 11 PC still freezes up, there is a reset option available. You can choose whether or not to save your data while restoring your machine to its original configuration.

Here's how to perform a hard restart of your computer:

- First, go to the Start menu, then click on Settings, System, Recovery, and finally, the Reset PC option.
- You can decide whether to save your files (which you'll probably want to do) or delete everything and start again.
- Follow the on-screen prompts to get your computer back in working order.

If you need to restore a Windows 11 installation, you can go back to running smoothly and securely using one of two common methods: a restore point or a system image backup. If your computer started crashing after installing new software, you can roll back to a previous restore point to fix it. To activate a restore point, set one up first. The good news is that you can use it to restore your system to a fully functional condition if you have one.

Here's how you can quickly create a system restore:

1. Click on the Start button, enter "restore point," and select the first result.
2. In the System Properties window, select the System Restore tab.
3. The Restore Point wizard can help you find a previous working state.
4. Use the Restore Point tool to implement the changes and restore your computer.

Keep in mind that this process will cause your computer to restart.

14.3 What to Do in Safe Mode

When Windows boots into Safe Mode, it uses just the bare minimum of system files and drivers. If a problem doesn't occur when booting into Safe Mode, it's likely unrelated to the system's default configuration or the standard drivers for installed devices. By observing Microsoft in Safe Mode, you may determine what is causing the issue and fix it more quickly.

Regarding Safe Modes, you can choose between the traditional Safe Mode and Safe Mode with Networking. You can access the internet and certain other devices on your network by booting into Safe Mode with Networking.

14.4 Leaving Safe Mode

To exit Safe Mode, simply restart your computer. The normal operating system should load after that. If restarting into Safe Mode persists, open System Configuration and deselect the "Safe boot" checkbox in the "Boot" tab's subset of Boot settings.

14.5 Windows Event Manager

The Windows Event Manager, also known as Event Viewer, is a system tool that is built into Windows and is designed to record and display operating system and application event messages. It enables system administrators to monitor system activity, troubleshoot problems, diagnose and correct system errors, and monitor system security. In essence, the Windows Event Manager helps users gain insight into what is happening on their Windows operating system. The Event Viewer may also be accessed in Windows 10 via the Settings menu in the Control Panel. To begin, open the Settings menu and go to System and Security. In Windows 11, the option to "View event logs" is still available at the bottom, but its location has been moved to Windows Tools. To launch the Microsoft Windows 11 Event Viewer, click on the link or press the corresponding shortcut. Alternatively, you can access the Windows Event Manager by typing "event" into the search bar in the Control Panel and selecting "View event logs."

14.6 Troubleshooting Connectivity Problem

Click on the Start menu, then go to Settings > System > Troubleshoot > Other. Under the "Other" menu, you can find Network Adapter > Run.

Try to resolve the issue by following the troubleshooting steps provided.

- First, power down your modem and wireless router, and then power them back up again. This will establish a new link with your ISP, but it may result in a temporary loss of connectivity for anyone currently using your Wi-Fi network. The basic procedures for restarting your modem and router are outlined below, although there may be some variations in the specifics:
- Disconnect the power cord to turn off the router.
- Some modem models come with backup batteries. If the modem's lights stay on after you turn off the power, try removing the device's battery.
- Wait for approximately 30 seconds.
- If you removed the modem's battery, put it back in. Make sure the modem is plugged back into the wall. The modem's indicator lights will flash, and the blinking must stop before you proceed.
- Reconnect the power cord to the back of your router. Allow the modem and router to fully boot up before proceeding. The devices usually have status LEDs indicating when they are ready.
- Retry your connection on your computer.

14.7 Keep your Windows 11 PC fast and performing

Performing a thorough and deep cleaning of your PC regularly (every 5-6 months) will help keep your PC healthy, and your operations will benefit significantly.

In fact, our computer is often slowed down by obsolete files that remain on our computer and which we may not even know exist during our daily activities. To ensure that our PC always runs at its full potential, we can use a program called CCleaner.

First go to **https://www.ccleaner.com/ccleaner/download** to download the latest free version available and then install it (you should have learned this process in previous chapters)

 WINDOWS 11 FOR SENIOR

Thank you for downloading CCleaner

Follow these **3 simple steps** to complete your **CCleaner** installation

Your download should start automatically within a few seconds.
If it doesn't, please use this link to <u>start the download</u>

When the program is installed, start it.

On the left side, you will find the various services that CCleaner offers you.

The two that you will need to use are:
1. Custom Clean
2. Performance Optimizer

Custom Clean
In this section, you can choose which obsolete files to delete, also differentiating them by the application to which they belong. Usually, when I do a deep clean, I prefer to select everything (both in Windows and Applications). Then, once you have selected what you want to delete, click on "Run Cleaner" to start the cleanup - it's a breeze!

Performance Optimizer
This section is very interesting. CCleaner will analyze your entire system and show you exactly what you can do to optimize your computer's performance, such as removing applications you no longer use, deleting unnecessary files, and more. The Performance Optimizer is one of the most useful tools that I often use when I need to optimize my clients' computers.

 WINDOWS 11 FOR SENIOR

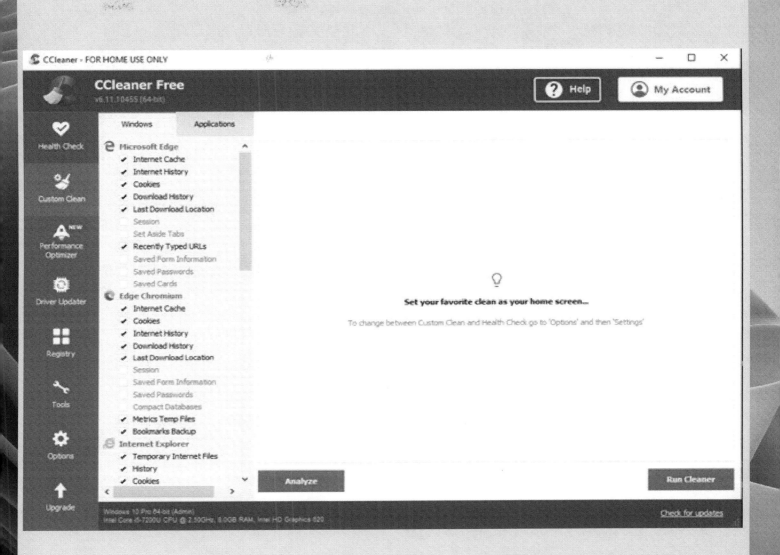

CCleaner - FOR HOME USE ONLY

CCleaner Free
v6.11.10455 (64-bit)

? Help

My Account

Health Check

Custom Clean

Performance Optimizer

Driver Updater

Registry

Tools

Options

Upgrade

Windows	Applications

- Microsoft Edge
  - ✔ Internet Cache
  - ✔ Internet History
  - ✔ Cookies
  - ✔ Download History
  - ✔ Last Download Location
  - Session
  - Set Aside Tabs
  - ✔ Recently Typed URLs
  - Saved Form Information
  - Saved Passwords
  - Saved Cards
- Edge Chromism
  - ✔ Internet Cache
  - ✔ Cookies
  - ✔ Internet History
  - ✔ Download History
  - ✔ Last Download Location
  - Session
  - Saved Form Information
  - Saved Passwords
  - Compact Databases
  - ✔ Metrics Temp Files
  - ✔ Bookmarks Backup
- Internet Explorer
  - ✔ Temporary Internet Files
  - ✔ History
  - ✔ Cookies

💡

Set your favorite clean as your home screen...

To change between Custom Clean and Health Check go to 'Options' and then 'Settings'

Analyze

Run Cleaner

Windows 10 Pro 64-bit (Admin)
Intel Core i5-7200U CPU @ 2.50GHz, 8.0GB RAM, Intel HD Graphics 620

Check for updates

 WINDOWS 11 FOR SENIOR

QUIZ
CHAPTER 14

1 - To boot into Safe Mode, press the key
A)   F2
B)   F3
C)   F4

2 - The sequence of ¬¬____ is important
A)   Recommendations
B)   Steps
C)   Errors

3 - If your Internet connection is not working, what can you do?
A)   Go into your PC's network settings and try restarting the modem
B)   Desperate
C)   Reboot the pc

The Windows Event manager may be launched quickly using a
A)   Control panel
B)   Search
C)   Taskbar

 WINDOWS 11 FOR SENIOR

5 - What does CCleaner allow you to do?
A)   Increase available RAM
B)   Increase the performance of your PC by analyzing and deleting obsolete files
C)   Restore deleted files

Answers
1.   C
2.   A
3.   A
4.   B
5.   B

WINDOWS 11 FOR SENIOR

CONCLUSION

We have reached the end of our journey, and I hope it has been satisfying, interesting, and full of insights for you. If so, it would be really important for me if you could leave a short review of a few lines about the book so that I can continue to grow and bring even better content on many more topics. As I mentioned, I would also like to create a very active community where users from all parts of the world can help each other. Please join the support Facebook group as well; here is the QR code to scan

 WINDOWS 11 FOR SENIOR

In this book, we have covered the most important topics, and now you should have the skills to start familiarizing yourself with this fantastic operating system.

We embarked on a journey through the evolution of Windows, starting from its initial version up to the latest release. Along the way, we explored the remarkable innovations introduced in each iteration, as well as identified their respective weaknesses.

We delved into the step-by-step process of upgrading our operating system to Windows 11, sharing some clever tricks to bypass compatibility checks on computers that may not meet the minimum requirements. Additionally, we covered the initial configuration of the OS, ensuring a smooth transition.

I introduced you to the prominent new features of Windows 11, with a special focus on the revamped File Explorer. We explored its organization and discussed how to leverage its functionalities to enhance our productivity. The Settings App received meticulous attention, highlighting its extensive customization options that allow us to tailor Windows 11 to our specific needs.

To optimize your workflow, I shared some time-saving tricks that I personally employ in my daily activities, such as utilizing the best keyboard shortcuts for tasks like copying, pasting, and text selection.

Windows 11 proves to be an incredibly robust and user-friendly operating system, offering a vast array of applications. I provided detailed analyses of popular web browsers, Chrome and Edge, ensuring you have a comprehensive understanding of their features and usage. We successfully configured our email accounts using the native Windows Mail App and comprehensively demonstrated how to create and send emails. Remember, there is an exercise awaiting you—to send me an email and practice your newfound skills.

We explored various methods of installing the software we need, whether it be through the convenient Microsoft Store or by seeking software online.

Ensuring your safety online was of utmost importance, and we discussed the significance of regular security updates. Additionally, we explored how to utilize our new operating system for entertainment purposes and how to seamlessly integrate it with our Android phones, allowing us to access our smartphone functionalities directly from our PCs.

Before we bid farewell, I would like to express my sincere gratitude for choosing my book. It would greatly assist me if you could spare a moment to leave a brief review on Amazon, as it will enable me to create more valuable content. If there's a specific topic that piques your interest, please let me know. If multiple readers share a common interest, I will eagerly begin crafting a book on that subject.

I thoroughly enjoy sharing my knowledge with others and I am excited to have you join my Facebook community. Together, we can continue to expand our understanding and engage in insightful discussions.

In addition, by scanning this QR code, you will gain access to a wealth of valuable resources, articles, and exclusive bonuses that I have curated just for you. This section is continuously updated, and you will also have the opportunity to subscribe to my newsletter. Rest assured, the newsletter will only contain relevant updates about new product features, security enhancements, and advanced notice of upcoming book releases. As a token of appreciation, you will have the privilege of receiving a sneak peek of my latest manuscript in exchange for your honest feedback. I guarantee that you will never receive any spam in your inbox.

 WINDOWS 11 FOR SENIOR

GLOSSARY

Account: The position of a user within a computer system that defines permissions for access and actions. Users log in to their accounts to gain access.

Antivirus: A program designed to detect and eliminate viruses present in files.

Attachment: A file that is included with a message, typically an email.

Browser: Client software used to view resources provided by a web server. Examples of browsers include Mozilla Firefox, Google Chrome, Opera, Safari, and Microsoft Internet Explorer.

Cache: A type of memory used to optimize data flow between devices with different access speeds.

CD-ROM: (Compact Disc Read-Only Memory) An optical storage medium derived from the music CD standard, modified for computer data storage. Most modern computers are equipped with a CD-ROM reader.

Client: An application that enables users to access services provided by a server. Web browsers are an example of clients.

CPU (Central Processing Unit): The central processing unit, which is the integrated circuit responsible for processing data.

 WINDOWS 11 FOR SENIOR

 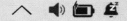

Default: The preset option chosen when more than one alternative is available.

Desktop: The workspace of a window manager where application windows are opened and displayed.

Directory: In a file system, a container that holds files and other directories (subdirectories).

Download: The process of transferring a file from a network to a computer.

Drag and drop: A technique available in graphical interface operating systems that involves dragging files or icons using the mouse.

Driver: Software that allows the operating system to manage a peripheral device.

Email: Electronic mail, which refers to messages sent through computers connected to the Internet.

File: Any item stored in the filesystem, such as text, images, sounds, programs, etc., distinguished by a name.

Firewall: Hardware or software that controls and filters data traffic between a network or host and the rest of the Internet to prevent unauthorized access and/or abuse.

Font: A complete set of characters with the same style, such as Arial or Times New Roman.

Hacker: A user with extensive knowledge of computers who is capable of discovering functionalities beyond the intended design of systems and identifying new security vulnerabilities.

Hard disk drive: A storage device installed inside a computer that stores data and programs. The contents are retained even when the computer is turned off. A physical drive can be divided into one or more user-defined partitions.

Hardware: Refers to all the tangible components of a computer, as opposed to software.

Hash: A function that generates a unique fixed-length string (hash value) from a file. This process is not reversible, meaning it is not possible to reconstruct the original file from the hash value. The hash serves as a "fingerprint" of the file, allowing its integrity to be verified at any time.

Icon: A small graphical representation on the desktop or in a graphical user interface (GUI) window that can be interacted with using the mouse pointer.

Input: Refers to the data entered into a program. Input devices are those that allow data to be entered into the computer.

Install: The process of creating and copying files and programs related to an application onto the hard disk.

Internet: The largest computer network that facilitates data exchange using the TCP/IP protocol. It is primarily achieved through telephone lines.

IP: Internet Protocol address that uniquely identifies a user and a computer connected to the Internet.

LAN: A local computer network that uses specialized connecting cables.

Login: The process by which an authenticated user is recognized by the system by entering a username and password during login.

Logoff: The opposite of login, referring to the act of exiting the system as a user. It can be done using the corresponding command.

 WINDOWS 11 FOR SENIOR

Modem: A device that enables the connection of two computer systems through a standard telephone line.

Monitor: An electronic device used for displaying images, text, and video transmitted in electronic format.

Mouse: A computer pointing device used for navigation and selection.

Multimedia: The presentation of data of various types (text, audio, video, etc.) within the same context.

Operating System: The essential software of a computer that allows it to be used. Without an operating system, a computer cannot function.

Output: Refers to the data produced by a program or the information displayed by a computer, as well as the peripherals used to present the results.

Password: A confidential code used to access secure resources and information.

Patch: A file that is designed to fix a bug or error in a software program.

Provider: A company that offers Internet connection services to customers.

RAM: This is the memory in which data is temporarily stored during processing. It is called volatile memory because it does not retain information when the computer is turned off.

Scanner: A device used to capture and convert images or printed text into digital format.

Software: A collection of programs that enable a computer to perform various tasks and functions.

Spam: Unsolicited electronic mail, typically of a commercial nature, that is sent in bulk to multiple users.

Virus: A program, usually with malicious intent, that can replicate itself by exploiting a system's resources and attaching itself to executable files.

Window manager: An application that enables user interaction with a computer through a graphical interface.

Wireless: A system of interconnection that operates without the use of wires, instead utilizing radio waves or, in some cases, infrared rays.

Made in United States
Troutdale, OR
08/05/2023

11849417R00144